TEX

Chico and Jefe

Cabeza de Vaca Lost in Texas

By Margot Spiekermann

Illustrated by Kristopher Gillespie

American Adventure Collection

Published by
American Legacy Publishing
1922 West 200 North
Lindon, Ut. 84042

Educators and librarians, for a variety of teaching tools, visit us at: www.americanadventurecollection.com

ISBN 0-9797909-1-3

Printed in China, September 2007

Unwelcome Stranger...

He felt a pang remembering how his mother always seasoned the roasted roots with wild garlic to cover their bitter taste. Waves of sadness flooded over him and his eyes grew misty. He missed his family so much. Then just as quickly, the sight of the stranger, Jefe, jolted him out of the memories and into the present. The sorrow evaporated and anger rushed back in.

Strengthened by that surge of anger, Chico promised himself again to survive, no matter what. If he had to live at his uncle's *ba-ak* with a stranger he hated, he'd do it until he could find a way out. He'd use the hate to keep himself going...

Book one in the Texas Adventure Series
from American Legacy Publishing

Chapter One

It really began with his dog.

He had a dog when he was twelve summers old. There were always plenty of dogs hanging around. A few were just wild scavengers, lurking at the edge of the camp for scraps. Others were trained to help with hunting and fishing. A good dog could scare up a flock of geese from the marsh grass, giving hunters plenty to aim at as the birds took flight. A good dog could retrieve the birds where they fell, or tree an opossum for an easy kill. Good dogs in a village worked for their living. They were valuable tools, just like spears and bows.

He knew his dog was different. It wandered into the village one day after wading across the marsh that separated the island from the mainland. They took to each other right away. The dog was scrawny and muddy and hungry all the time. It did plenty of oddball things too, like chewing on rocks and chasing gulls and licking at the foam left where the waves met the beach. The adults said the dog was useless. They yelled at it the same way they yelled at the boy for playing when he should be working.

The dog could spend a whole morning pawing wet holes in the sand and trying to catch the tiny crabs that scuttled along the tide line. And the boy could spend all morning just watching him. Sometimes the dog would finally catch a crab and manage to crunch it up before it could pinch his tongue with its little claws. Other times the boy would hear a yelp and then he would laugh as he watched the dog shaking its head to loosen the little crab's grasp.

It was a plain brown dog that never stopped running around except to collapse with its master on his sleeping mat at night. It didn't really seem to be very smart or very useful, but it was the boy's companion. It was always at his side. And it was there at the very beginning.

That day, the dog acted especially strange. It ran up and down the beach, barking at the waves. It looked at the boy as if it were frustrated; as if the boy couldn't understand what the animal was trying to show him. It's true, the sea was choppy and angry, slapping wave against wave, but the dog usually wouldn't pay more than a moment's attention to that. Today, though, the animal could not seem to tear itself away.

The boy studied the autumn sky, trying to ignore the barking by watching the clouds swirling overhead. The seasons were changing. A storm was brewing somewhere out over the water, and everything around seemed restless, as though waiting for something. The dune grasses bent close against the sand with every gust of wind. The gulls swooped high and then low, flying into each other, shrieking and agitated.

Even the tide couldn't seem to decide just how far to roll up on the beach. The boy watched as one wave barely touched the shore before slipping back. Then the next one raced further and further across the wet sand, stretching thinner and thinner until it finally ran out and just sank into the earth.

Nature herself seemed out of sorts. It was no wonder the dog felt anxious.

"Make him stop, Son," Behma paused to comment as

he passed. "That dog is going to drive every last bird and turtle and rabbit back to the mainland." Then he turned and headed into the dunes to check his hunting snares.

Behma was a man of few words. When he spoke at all, everyone knew he meant what he said.

The boy tried to obey his father, but the dog wouldn't leave that stretch of beach all afternoon. Sometimes he managed to get it to stop barking long enough to sit next to him for a moment. But even then it just kept staring out toward the horizon and whimpering.

Other men came and went. Some of them would grunt a greeting as they passed. Others glared disapprovingly at the pair. A couple of friends, boys his age, stopped to talk.

"Look what we found!" one of them boasted. "Turtle eggs! My dog sniffed out an old nest down at the end of the dunes. Can you believe it, this late in the season?"

The boy admired their find and they talked a while before he decided to give up trying to quiet his dog. He started to go back to help his mother gather the last wild garlic, a chore he was supposed to have been doing all day. But then he caught sight of something far out on the water. It appeared to float on top of the waves, like a boat, but he was sure none of the villagers would take their canoes out into the open sea. Occasionally one might risk the danger, gambling on a big fish catch, but he knew that not even a foolish man would dare venture out into these angry waters.

He stood for a long time, his hand shading his eyes from the glare. The sun was beginning to set behind him, and the light reflecting on the water made him squint. He watched the object bounce on the distant surf. A few minutes passed before he realized the dog had stopped barking.

"Son!" He heard his mother, Kaninma, call, punctuated by a couple of shrill whistles.

The dog looked up. It muttered a quiet "woof," but stayed rooted next to the boy. The boy chuckled and scratched its head, and they both stayed right where they were, gazing out to sea.

The boy's eyes began to water from staring so hard. He didn't want to miss anything, but finally he had to shake his head and look away. Squatting down next to the dog, he wrapped his arms around his knees and watched a wave sneak up and tickle his toes for a moment while his eyesight cleared. When he was able to focus again on the distant object, he could tell that it was coming closer toward his island, but it was still too far away to make out any real details.

"Son!" he heard Kaninma call again. Then she whistled sharply. "Come right now!"

He jumped up and ran all the way to the *ba-ak*, the small hut where the boy lived with his family. His parents, Behma and Kaninma, and his sister, Kada, already crouched by the small fire inside. The warmth seeping out the doorway felt good against his skin. He'd been watching the horizon so intently that he hadn't noticed the growing chill in the gusty winds. Nor had he noticed the hungry knot in his stomach until the aroma of bubbling soup set his mouth watering. The dog was hungry, too. It scurried off, sniffing around the *ba-ak* for scraps or bones that Kaninma might have tossed out while she prepared the food.

Kaninma was stirring the fire's embers when her son entered, breathless and excited. The fish and clam soup would be delicious. The rising steam meant he'd probably burn his fingers when he dipped out the clamshells, but the tasty morsel of meat inside each one would be worth it.

"Sit," Behma ordered, pointing at the space next to Kada. His father's face was expressionless, but that wasn't unusual. Behma smiled every once in a while, especially over a fine catch of fish, but rarely was a smile directed at his son.

The boy sat.

The family ate the meal silently. Like his dog earlier, now the boy fidgeted, bursting to tell about the strange object he'd seen floating toward their island. He wanted his father to know that something interesting was happening, something out of the ordinary. He wanted to hurry back to the beach to wait and watch, but he kept still and silent. It was not the Karankawa way to hold conversations while eating.

A sudden rush of wind made the hut's deer hide walls flap. He rubbed his arms for warmth and inched a little closer to the fire. It would feel good to have his dog lying next to him tonight when they slept. The dog was warm, and it blocked the wind on nights like this.

Behma looked at his son and jerked his head toward the roof. "Storms come. Bring extra firewood inside tonight where it won't get wet from the rains." Then he turned to Kada. "Set extra containers outside to catch the rainwater."

Water and fire. These were the two essential tools for survival. Food could be hunted. Tools could be crafted. But fire and fresh water? Those meant the difference between life and death. The children didn't need to be told twice to get busy. Other things, no matter how exciting or mysterious, would have to wait.

Their father rose and left the hut, taking his spearing stick with him. Certain fish lay flat in the shallows at the other end of the island. These were best hunted at night. To catch them, Behma would shuffle through knee-deep water to disturb the fish where they rested in the sand. Then he'd easily spear them right at his feet as they tried to swim away in confusion. His young son wasn't very good yet at most kinds of hunting, but he loved to help Behma catch these slow-moving fish.

"Father," the boy called after Behma as he walked away from the hut. "I'll come help you as soon as I gather the wood!"

In answer, Behma raised the arm that held his spear, never pausing or turning. He kept walking down the path, but his son knew by his gesture that he'd heard him, and the youngster hurried to finish his chore.

It seemed to take forever to gather up enough wood for the next day's fire. There wasn't much nearby, so he had to scramble through the dunes looking for driftwood. He found a few dead limbs broken from some scrubby trees, plus an armful of dried up fan-shaped leaves blown from the palm trees beyond the village. Finally, sure that he'd gathered enough to keep them supplied with fuel for the next day, the boy ran to join his father.

A chill raced through him as he left the hut. He shivered, but didn't know why. He'd worked up a sweat picking up the firewood, but he felt cold through and through. The dog appeared out of nowhere and licked his hand, and he felt better.

He was excited about helping his father catch fish. But he was also anxious to see if the floating object had landed yet on the beach. He'd be disappointed if it turned out to be nothing more than a mirage, a trick of light and shadows from the sunset's glare.

The moon had risen at sunset. It was huge and white, suspended in the sky like a giant pearl. The moonlight was so bright that it took a while before he noticed the fires far down the beach, at the distant end of the island. But once he did finally see them, he couldn't wait to know what was going on. Surely Behma and the other men hadn't lit fires just for an evening of fishing.

The boy began to run down the long stretch of sand, his bare feet slapping on the wet ground. His dog ran right beside him and its feet kicked up little sprays of brown sand.

Stopping at the top of the last dune to catch his breath, he studied the scene before him. Dozens of men lay sprawled around three big bonfires, yet it was totally quiet except for the usual evening sounds of the surf and the wind and the gulls. He thought he could make out his father's tall silhouette, along with others from the village, moving carefully among the groups, bending close to gesture or lend a hand.

At first glance he couldn't tell who the people were,

lying there silently on the sand. But after a while, his eyes adjusted to the flickering firelight and the shadowy moonlight. The people were definitely strangers. They didn't look at all like the villagers. They were shorter, and their pale skin looked blotchy, perhaps blistered or sunburned. They wore strange bits of cloth. There were no paintings or piercings on their faces or bodies. Even from a distance, they appeared exhausted and battered, as if they'd been beaten up by the violent waves.

The boy couldn't help wondering what had happened and why they were there. Why did they choose to land on this beach? Had they simply been blown off course? Were they what he'd seen earlier, floating far out on the waves? Were they traders? But where were their boats that carried the goods? He looked around and saw nothing more than a some of piles of debris, probably just driftwood and branches tangled with sea mosses blown in by the billowing winds. Maybe their boats had washed away in the angry tides.

If they weren't traders, who else might they be? In their condition, they posed no threat if they were a conquering tribe. There was no reason for anybody to want to take over the village anyway. It was no secret that the little Karankawa band had nothing except what they used from day to day. Their possessions were few, they lived off the land, and the land belonged to everyone.

Why were the strangers there? Where had they come from?

The native boy was puzzled, somehow disappointed, and oddly disturbed by the day's events. The sight in front of him was certainly not what he'd expected. He stood staring in the half-dark, trying to figure it out. His dog, so frantic all day, now stayed quiet and close to his side.

Behma saw his son and beckoned. Surprised to be noticed, the boy hurried across the sand at his father's signal, picking his way through the quiet clusters of men.

Chapter 2

If the boy hadn't seen with his own eyes that these were actually men lying on the sand, he'd have thought it was the site of a big fish kill.

Sometimes, after big storms, great stretches of the beach were covered in dead fish. The fish would drown in the swirling water far out at sea, and then get swept in by the tides. He thought that was how these men looked. Most were sprawled around, limp, their bodies at all angles.

Some even looked dead. The only movement came from their faint breathing. Most seemed too weak to even moan.

"Ugh," the boy muttered, wrinkling his nose. "Smells like rotting fish." The odor made him feel sick.

The dog was repulsed too. It stopped to sniff at one man and lick his face. Then it turned away, whimpering.

The boy's uncle, Yamawe, had joined Behma, and they appeared to be having a serious conversation. Yamawe was much younger than Behma and had recently taken a wife, Hamala. The boy didn't like his new aunt. She was beautiful, but she was vain about her looks, and she talked rudely to the other women and children of the village. As much as possible she avoided the drudgery of women's work, and instead expected her new husband to provide everything she wanted. She was very demanding, and the boy resented her because she took away the attention his uncle used to give him. He was relieved to see Yamawe out alone tonight. The boy moved near his uncle, hoping to be noticed.

Yamawe smiled when he saw his nephew, but then turned serious again. He pointed down the beach at the debris the boy had noticed earlier. "Go see what's left of their boats. They broke up in the waves and the men were cast out on the shore. Drag whatever you can find up onto the dunes where it won't wash away. They'll need their supplies to continue their journey."

He couldn't believe what his uncle was saying. It was plain to him there was nothing left worth saving.

He didn't have a good feeling about it, but he hurried to do what Yamawe told him. It was not Karankawa custom to question one's elders, even when a task seemed like a waste of time.

One of the boy's friends came, too. Mano was one of the boys who had bragged about finding the turtle eggs that afternoon. Now he was just as puzzled as his friend was. Their dogs sniffed around the soggy rubbish and tugged together on a piece of rotten animal hide. It fell apart at the touch of their teeth.

"No good." Mano kicked at the mess and shook his head. Like most of the village natives, he used words sparingly.

There wasn't much else to be found, so the two friends gathered all the broken pieces of wood and laid them to dry for firewood. They tossed the long strands of seaweed aside but didn't uncover anything more than scraps of tattered hides and bits of cloth. Even after searching up and down the beach, they couldn't find anything else to salvage. Every last thing these strangers had brought had been destroyed or washed away by the stormy waves.

From what the two young Karankawa boys saw, not only did the strangers smell bad, but they were completely helpless as well. And now, because they'd ended up stranded on this village's beach, their helplessness had become the village's problem. It didn't matter if they wanted the strangers to stay or leave, the villagers would have to help. It was their way.

Giving up, the two boys whistled for their dogs and turned back. When they reached the bonfires, Mano stopped and pointed, "Look at that!"

The women of the village had come to the beach. They gathered among the men, and bent over the strangers. The whole group, villagers and strangers alike, sat crying together.

It seemed as though they were on the beach for a long time. The moon hung silently over the misery on the beach. The night grew dark, but it remained easy to tell the different people apart. The Karankawa men, like Behma and Yamawe, were much taller than the shipwrecked men. Even crouching together beside the fire, they towered above the shorter sailors. The sailors appeared uncomfortable and ashamed of their bare skin, while the village hunters proudly wore only short breechcloths at their waists and piercings on their chests. The boy recognized his mother, Kaninma among the other women. She sat in her long moss skirt, brushing the wet hair from the eyes of one of the strangers.

The differences among the people were obvious to him. And yet he found that when he blinked, the whole gathering seemed to blur together before his eyes. They blended into just a single group, joined in one cause, mourning for the sailors' lost hope.

If the strangers hadn't yet figured out how hopeless their situation was, then surely they knew now, he thought. There was nothing the villagers could offer them except their tears. They couldn't rebuild their boats. They couldn't raise their dead. They couldn't even understand each other's language. They could only communicate by weeping together.

"What do you think is going to happen?" he asked Mano.

Mano shrugged.

The two friends quietly slipped into the gathering and squatted beside their fathers, but the boy couldn't make himself join in and cry for the strangers. They were going to be a lot of trouble. He just knew it.

After half an hour of crying, people gradually began to quiet down. The boy felt impatient. He couldn't see that the tears had solved any problems, and his legs had cramped from sitting so long in the chilly air. The dog poked at his master's hand with its wet nose, trying to get him to go play.

"Not now," the boy whispered, sneaking in a quick scratch behind its ear so it knew he wasn't mad, and then pushing the dog away. It gave a little "yip" and then bounded off to chase toads in the dune grass. "Sure wish I could go run around, too," the bored youngster thought to himself.

The wind picked up and the dampness in the air turned to a fine mist. He was relieved to see Behma stand up to speak. As usual, the tall leader got right to the point. "These men are weak. We must get them to the village before the storm comes."

People nodded in agreement. Finally, all the crying stopped and the band of villagers started to get up. The strangers couldn't understand what Behma had said, but they'd seen him gesturing at them.

Another boy elbowed Mano. "Look how scared they are. They look like they think we're planning to eat them or something."

Mano laughed and returned the joke. "Ha! They're too bony for that!"

The friends all chuckled together, but deep down the boy did wish he could make the sailors understand they were safe. They were guests, and it was Karankawa tradition to treat guests like family. He sometimes wondered if it was a foolish custom to bring uninvited strangers into their homes, but he was only a child and it was not his place to question the judgment of the elders. Still, he would have liked for the worried sailors to know they had nothing to fear.

"Come, Kada. There is much to do," Kaninma said to her daughter. They rose quietly and led the rest of the women back to the village to get ready.

The boys' eyes brightened at the thought of food. That was one custom every young Karankawa did like. The villagers honored any guests with celebration and feasting. It was how they showed respect for visitors, welcoming them with food and hospitality, sharing everything they had. While the women got the cooking fires ready, several boys were sent to check the fish traps, and the little girls went to dig clams. There would be plenty of food ready by the time the strangers arrived at the little cluster of huts.

Behma handed his son a torch from the bonfire, and gave another to Mano. "Make fires between here and the village," he told them. "We'll have to stop often to let these men rest and warm up along the way."

The two friends looked at each other and grinned. "This is the best job of all!" the boy whispered to Mano. "We'll get to watch everybody as they pass along the trail from beginning to end!"

It wasn't a very long walk up the island, but Behma was right. The shipwrecked men had a hard time. Some of them had to be carried, and even the ones who could walk were very slow. They were all too thin and too pale, as if they'd been suffering for a long time before they ever washed up on the beach. In the moonlight, they looked like a band of skeletons marching slowly along the silent sands.

The moon had drifted past its highest point by the time the group finally straggled into the village. The boys had to work hard to keep the fires burning in the stormy wind and dampness, but they managed.

"Father!" the boy called out as Behma trudged past. "Is that the last of them?"

A sailor leaned heavily against the village leader. Behma raised his fishing spear with his free arm, just as he'd done hours ago, before the strangers had washed up on the beach. The boys were tending the last fire–the one closest to the village. Behma turned and nodded, smiling, as he passed the boys. That rare smile revived his son the same way the warm fires revived the exhausted men. Their job done, the two friends whistled for their dogs and followed the last men into the village.

The village was alive with light and noise. Flames leaped in the central fire pit, burning strong and protected from the wind. The aroma of boiling fish soups and steaming crabs hung in the damp air. Drums echoed, shell bracelets clattered, neighbors called out to each other. Firewood popped and crackled. Gulls shrieked overhead, anxious to scoop up an overlooked clam or fishtail.

It was a scene full of celebration and welcome, but the visitors seemed terrified. Every family looked after two or three of them. The sailors ate as if they were starving. They acted exhausted and fearful.

The villagers began a great celebration that lasted all night long. Besides dancing and music, there was drinking and feasting. There were wrestling contests and shooting competitions. Yamawe was the best wrestler in the village. He easily pinned every opponent who challenged him as his nephew and Mano cheered, whooping and punching the air with their fists in excitement. Later, Behma won the shooting competition by shooting his arrow the farthest of any man there.

Yamawe clapped his nephew on the back and told him, "One day maybe you'll be half the hunter your father is!" The boy smiled proudly, but worried a little that he'd ever be able to live up to such high expectations.

The strangers huddled together near the largest *ba-ak*. Occasionally they whispered nervously to each other, but most of the evening they simply watched, wide-eyed. At the time, the boy thought the strangers were too scared and tired to join in.

It turned out to be something completely different.

—

The boy groaned when he opened his eyes the next morning. The hard rain had started at dawn and was coming down in sheets. The wind had blown steadily colder and colder through the night.

"He smells!" were the first words out of his mouth. He couldn't help complaining. The stench from the sailor lying next to him made the boy gag, and he was trapped inside the dank, smoky hut.

"When are they leaving?" he whined to his father.

"When they're able," Behma answered. The boy didn't think that answer was helpful at all.

As the day wore on, the smell bothered him more and more. The stranger just lay there on a deer hide that was soggy from the rain seeping in under the walls. He had beads of sweat on his forehead even though the wind still blew cold. When Behma tried to talk to him with hand gestures and sign language, the man just closed his eyes and ignored him.

For days it was like that. Rain outside, coughing and stench inside. His family spoke little. The stranger spoke not at all.

Finally, the rain slowed down and the boy scrambled outside with his dog.

"It's cold but at least we can breathe," he said, scratching the dog behind the ear while they gulped the fresh air. Without warning, the dog took off running.

"Where's he going this time?" Mano called, as he joined his friend. They watched the dog racing down to the beach, bouncing over clumps of grass, and stopping to roll around in the wet sand.

"Looks like he's trying to get away from the smell!" The boy laughed.

"The two strangers in our hut are sick," Mano said. "I couldn't stand it any more. I don't care if the storms come back, I'm staying outside."

"Really? Yours are sick, too?" the boy asked. "Ours just lays there and ignores us."

They walked together down to the beach. The dog stood barking at the waves, nipping at the foam that reached its toes. The boys started to wander toward the end of the island where the strangers had washed ashore. More bits and pieces of cloth and a few broken wood planks had washed up in the night's storm. When the boys began to head toward those, the dog growled.

The dog had never growled at him before. The boy took another step toward the remains. More growls. Then the dog started barking and racing around in circles. It seemed intent on keeping the boys away from the debris.

"That's one strange dog," Mano shook his head. "What's it so worked up about?"

"I don't know. I've never seen it act this way before," the puzzled boy answered. "Sometimes I can't figure it out. Let's just go back."

"Yeah. I've got a stomach ache," Mano agreed. "Must be from the long night."

In fact, Mano looked queasy by the time they got close to the village. The dog calmed down when the two boys turned toward home, but it never left their side on the walk back. It acted determined to lead them away from the shipwreck litter on the beach.

"Hey, Mano, are you sure you can make it?" the boy asked. His friend looked completely worn out from the walk. "Did you eat some bad oysters last night? Or did you just stay up too late?"

Mano started to laugh, then clutched his stomach and winced. "Something like that," he said, gritting his teeth. He bent over. "Wait," he held up a hand. "Wait for me to catch my breath."

It was a good thing they were almost home because the boy wasn't sure his friend could make it much farther. He let Mano lean on him for support. Mano was the bigger of the two, and it took all of the smaller boy's strength. Mano's forehead was wet when they reached his hut. His friend told him it was only raindrops.

But he was wrong.

That was the way the sickness started. In a few days, there wasn't a hut in the village that didn't have at least one sick person. And once there was sickness in a hut, everyone in that family caught it. And when the whole family was sick, there was no one well enough to care for the others.

It began with stomach cramps–stomach cramps and great weariness. There was pain, fever, and filth. It seemed no one was healthy enough to clean up the waste or cool the fever or quench the raging thirst. The villagers began to die. So did the sailors. Within days most of them were gone.

Looking back later, the boy wondered if the sickness had spread because they had all stayed together–if they had slept outside instead of cooped up together in the bad air, would more of them have survived? Maybe the illness came from sharing the damp deerskin blankets. Or maybe it was a bad season for the few oysters they'd just started gathering. Or maybe, he thought, just maybe, the strangers had brought the illness with them.

The sailor who slept in Behma's *ba-ak* suffered and moaned for three long, miserable days. He coughed and retched and got weaker and weaker. Kaninma and Kada tried to feed and clean him; Behma tried to help the man get up and walk. And the boy just tried to stay out of the way. He used any excuse to go outside.

"I'll get more firewood," he'd announce as he and his dog hurried away. They wandered the dunes and checked the fish traps several times a day. His parents were so busy taking care of the stranger that they didn't notice how much time the boy spent away from the hut.

None of it made any difference. The stranger finally died, and then the rest of the family, including the boy, caught the sickness.

Behma returned from burying the sailor. At first, he tried to hide his stomachache from the others. His son saw the pain in his eyes, though, and it wasn't long before Behma broke out in a feverish sweat.

"Bring me water, Son," he said wearily and gave the boy one last small smile. By the next day all he could do was grit his teeth and clench his eyes shut as painful cramps wracked his strong body. Kaninma, Kada and the boy tried to comfort him, but one by one they all got sick and everything turned into a horrible, dizzy nightmare.

The boy's whole family died. He was too weak to help his parents and sister while they were sick, and there was no one to bury them when they died. In the end, he decided he had no choice. He crawled from the hut and threw a burning torch inside before he collapsed, sobbing and exhausted, in the sand.

A few days earlier the boy's world had been quiet and familiar, his family strong and close around him. He was Behma and Kaninma's son. He was Kada's brother. He was Mano's friend. Now he watched helplessly as that world went up in smoke.

The dog stayed with him. He never knew how many nights he lay outside the smoking remains of the *ba-ak*, but every time he opened his eyes, the dog was beside him. The rain washed his dirty body clean, the winds cooled his fever, and the dog kept him warm. All the boy could do was sleep, but the dog stayed and kept him warm. He didn't eat or speak or move for days, but still the dog stayed and kept him warm.

He was feverish and starving and scared. He lay there, alone with his dog, wanting to die like the others. He knew he couldn't survive by himself. He was no longer a child, but he was not yet a man who could live on his own. And he'd lost everything, just like the sailors who had shipwrecked on the beach.

He was ready to give up. He wished that he could let himself go to sleep and never wake up. The boy slept. But as he slept, the storm died out, and sweet healing winds blew over him instead.

And in his dreams, the boy knew that he was going to live.

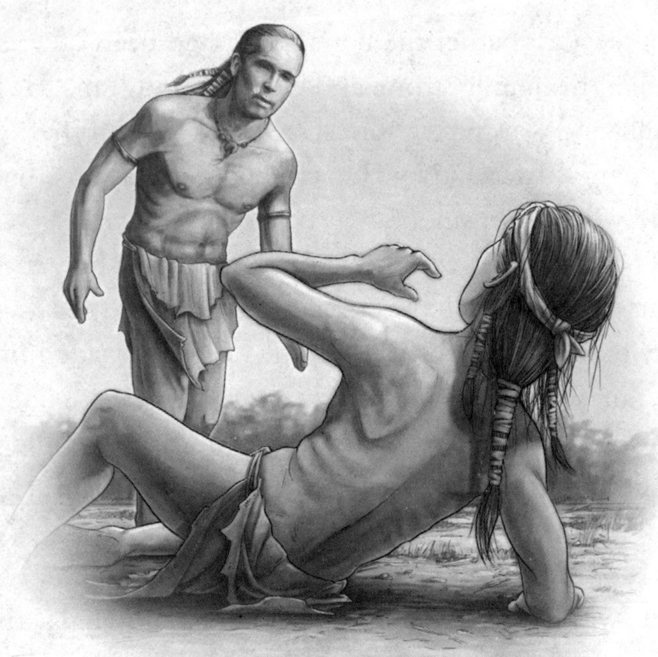

Chapter 3

The dog licked the boy's face.

He pushed himself up on his elbows and wondered why it made his head spin when he tried to look around. Then he remembered everything. The shipwreck, the storms, the sickness, the death. He closed his eyes, hoping to make it all go away, but the dog started licking his face again.

"Yip!" it insisted.

He opened his eyes again. He started to push the dog

away, but then he looked at its face. Its ears lay back flat against its head and its eyes were stretched wide. Instead of white, the dog's eyeballs were ringed with yellow. It panted softly with its mouth slightly open, and its breath came in short, tired bursts.

"Have you been sick, too, dog?" he asked. His voice sounded raspy and dry. Just reaching to scratch the dog's head sapped his energy. He lay back, panting, and forced himself to think.

He remembered the storms. He recalled how the sky had been so dark with clouds that it was hard to tell day from night. Sometimes flashes of lightning had lit up the darkness. Great claps of thunder followed, and rumbled away into the distance.

He remembered hearing the wild crashing of waves against the beach just beyond the dunes that protected the village. The powerful pounding of the surf and the crashing thunder came together with such violence that even the ground vibrated. He wondered if that was why he'd dreamed about dozens of drums beating and echoing around him while he was sick.

Now the air was cold, and the sun shone brightly. The boy wondered if the storms had passed. The wind and rain had stopped. The flames from the burning hut had gone out, but deep in the big pile of ashes were embers that still smoldered and gave off heat. He inched closer. Again he panted from the exertion, but he was glad to feel the warmth.

"Yip," the dog barked again. It sat with its back toward the boy and whimpered a little, just as it had that day on the beach when the strangers' boats were floating on the horizon. The boy paid attention. He wondered if someone was out there who could help him.

He got back up on one elbow and looked in the same direction the dog was staring. Everything seemed normal at first. A skinny dog sniffed around a cold fire pit. Seagulls circled high in the sky, calling loudly to each other. But then he began to notice changes. Where were all the huts? Only one or two were left where the boy remembered they'd been, and there were many empty spaces. Mounds of sand seemed to have grown in their places.

Then he understood. Those mounds were graves. Other families had buried their dead before packing each *ba-ak* and leaving. The village looked empty now.

Because the families in a Karankawa band moved from place to place to hunt for food, they never stayed in one area very long. They took their huts with them when they left. A *ba-ak* was easy to put up and take down because it was made of deer hides hung on a simple frame of willow branches. Sometimes a *ba-ak* was covered with grass mats or even big palm leaves instead of animal hides, depending on the weather. And now the boy saw that nearly all of the villagers had packed up their homes and moved on.

"Where have they gone?" he asked out loud. Talking out loud made him realize how thirsty he was. He licked his lips and tried to think.

The dog glanced at him and weakly thumped its tail. Then it turned back and stared into the distance. It gave a couple of short barks before the boy noticed what it had sighted. Far at the other end of the village was a bit of smoke. A person stooped near a fire, probably adding wood and stirring the coals. Then he stood up and turned the boy's direction.

"Here!" The boy tried to wave his arm. His voice came out weak. "I'm still here!"

How could he get the person's attention? It might be the only person left in the village. The boy was frantic. He needed help. He saw his father's fishing spear on the ground near him where it had blown away from the hut in the storm. He had to crawl to reach it. He clutched it at one end and waved it as high as he could. The dog added a few weak barks.

Finally, the man looked right at them. He shouted something and started their direction.

"Here!" The boy cried again in a weak voice. "Help!"

As the man drew closer, the boy recognized his uncle,

Yamawe. He was tall, like Behma, athletic, quick, and agile. Yamawe didn't move very gracefully or quickly now, though. He stumbled as he walked. He appeared sick or exhausted, but the boy didn't care. He was just glad to know he wasn't alone.

"Nephew!" Yamawe cried, sinking to his knees when he reached the sick boy. The nephew reached out and grasped his uncle's arm, but said nothing.

"I am so glad to see you," Yamawe continued when he caught his breath. "I thought you were gone. I saw your hut catch fire days ago."

The youngster was quiet. He didn't know what to tell him. He didn't know where to start.

"You got the sickness, too?" Yamawe prompted him.

His nephew nodded.

"Your family?" he asked softly.

The boy nodded again. It hurt too much to say it out loud.

Yamawe studied his nephew's suffering face. Finally he rolled back and stared up at the sky.

"I am not as sick as Hamala, your aunt" Yamawe told him. "I don't know why not. The two sailors staying with us got sick. One died. The other just sleeps. And Hamala is still very sick with cramps and fever," he didn't finish.

"What happened?" the nephew asked after a long

silence.

"What do you remember?" his uncle asked in return.

"I remember the celebration, and the storms starting," the boy whispered. He closed his eyes to concentrate. "I remember people getting tired and weak and then the stomach sickness. Everybody in our hut had it, and we were all too weak to take care of each other." He swallowed. "They all died but me, and I couldn't do anything. I couldn't call for help. I couldn't bury them. So I took a stick from the fire and burned the hut." He stopped again because he didn't want to cry.

Then he took a breath and went on. He struggled to make his voice sound normal. "My dog and I just lay here until we saw you this morning. I don't know how much time has passed or where everyone has gone," he ended with a shrug. He was out of breath from so much talking. He waited and hoped his uncle could tell him what had happened.

Yamawe shook his head. "It has been many days since we found the strangers on our beach. The sickness struck everyone: sailors and villagers, young and old. Most of our people who survived decided to leave. They went to join another village across the inlet on the next island. One of the sailors in my *ba-ak* is still alive, though, and I decided to stay and care for him. He is still very sick and I couldn't just leave him to die alone. And now that my wife is sick, I don't really care what happens to me."

"So there is no one else left?"

"There are a few others who are living out in the dunes, hoping they won't get sick if they stay away from the village. They may be right. I don't know," Yamawe said.

"I think the strangers brought the sickness," his nephew suggested, feeling bitter. He lay flat on his back and clenched a fist in weak frustration. "Maybe they use sickness like a weapon to conquer other people. Maybe they came to destroy us."

The boy needed to think about that, but he was so tired. He thought the pain he felt would make more sense if he could just blame somebody for it. He closed his eyes again.

"In a way, it's the strangers' fault, even if they didn't bring the sickness," he said after a long pause.

"How can that be true?" Yamawe asked.

"If they hadn't come, we wouldn't have held our celebration and the sickness wouldn't have spread," his nephew answered, propping himself up again on one elbow.

"And if the storms hadn't caused the strangers to shipwreck, they wouldn't have come to our island at all," Yamawe explained. He shrugged and added, "Maybe it is their fault. Maybe it isn't. Nephew, you just have to accept that we can't always understand how or why some things happen."

The man didn't saying anything else for a long time. Then he sighed and asked, "Would you like some water?"

The weary boy licked his dry lips and nodded.

Yamawe reached over and squeezed his nephew's shoulder. Then he heaved himself up with a grunt and said, "I'll be back soon with something to drink." He leaned to scratch the dog's head and then headed back across what was left of the village.

The boy lay back and watched his uncle trudge slowly down the path. The sun had risen high in the sky. Shadows danced on the ground where the clumps of dune grasses blew in the gentle breeze. The air smelled salty and fresh and clean. He turned his head. Behma's fishing spear still lay where he had dropped it after signaling Yamawe. He strained to reach it. It was warm because it had been lying in the sun, and his fingers clutched it tightly.

"Father," he murmured, remembering what had happened since that day the strangers came. He wondered what would happen next.

It wasn't long before Yamawe came back with water. He carried it in a tall, narrow jug made of tightly woven marsh grass. The inside had been smeared with some of the black tar that often washed up on the beach. That layer of tar sealed the basket and kept it from leaking

The water felt good in the boy's dry mouth and throat. His hands were shaky, so he drank it clumsily and a lot dribbled down his chin. He didn't care because that felt good, too. After he caught his breath, he held some water in his hand and let the dog take a drink. It lapped up the water, not stopping until it licked the boy's hand completely dry.

"I must get back to the others," Yamawe announced when they finished drinking. "Rest a while and then see if you can walk to my hut."

His nephew took a deep breath. The water had helped him feel much better, but he knew he was very weak. "I'm not sure I can make it on my own," he told his uncle.

"You have to try. There is nothing left for you here," Yamawe said bluntly. "I want to help you, but the others are very sick and need me to stay with them. If you don't make it by dark, I'll bring a torch and look for you. Just stay on the path where the walking is easiest and you'll be fine."

Then he left and the boy was alone again with only his dog.

He sat and watched Yamawe go without another word. "There is nothing left for you here," his uncle had said. The boy looked at the ruins of the burned-out hut he had shared with his family. It was true. There was nothing left for him here.

Bewildered, he lay back on the ground again. He couldn't imagine what he was going to do next. He used his arm to shade his eyes from the sun, and tried to focus his thoughts.

He was scared and sad, and the fear and the grief paralyzed him. He felt trapped and helpless, and alone. He wanted desperately to get away from here, get away from the fear and sadness, but he didn't think he had the strength to even move.

He clenched his fists in frustration. He was angry and he wanted to blame somebody for his troubles. He wanted to make somebody pay for causing his problems. He wanted to make someone else suffer and feel scared and sad, too. And suddenly, without understanding why, he realized that being angry made him want to get up and do something.

The boy knew then that anger was the tool he needed to keep going.

It seemed like a good solution at the time. It gave him a reason to pull himself up and move. He held on to his anger as tightly as he held his father's fishing spear. He leaned on them both for the strength to take just one more step. And step by angry step, he managed the whole trip across the village by the time the sun set.

For the hundredth time, he stopped to catch his breath, and then started to move the last few steps to the fire outside Yamawe's *ba-ak*. The sky was clear that night and the sun left a purplish-pink glow as it slipped behind the marshes at the back of the island. A group of pelicans floated above, their big beaks pointed toward the beach. The boy always thought they were funny looking birds, and he liked to follow after them and watch them dive into the waves for the small fish that swam close to the surface. When one caught a fish, it tipped its head back with its beak pointed straight up. With a quick shake, the fish slid right down the pelican's long throat. It made the boy laugh every time.

He didn't have the energy to follow the birds tonight, though. Even his burning new anger couldn't carry him much farther. Yamawe stepped around the side of his hut just as his nephew reached the end of the path. He smiled wearily.

"I knew you could do it," Yamawe said simply.

"Well, I did," his nephew snapped back. He was exhausted and thirsty and Yamawe hadn't even offered to help him sit. Instead, Yamawe gave him an order.

"Take this water inside to the stranger. His fever has broken and he's thirsty."

Chapter 4

The boy stared at Yamawe. He could not believe what he'd just heard.

Yamawe was ordering him to look after a sick stranger—one of the strangers responsible for killing half the village? "This is too much!" the boy longed to cry out. His whole family was dead because of this man, and Yamawe expected him to help the filthy stranger? The young Karankawa knew it was not his place to argue with an adult, but

Yamawe's words raised up a fierce anger in him.

He leaned heavily on his father's spear. Yamawe handed his nephew the full jug of water, but the boy was too weak to hold on to it. His knees buckled, the water fell and spilled, and the tired boy crumpled to the ground. His dog eagerly lapped up the water pouring across the sand.

Yamawe sighed, exasperated. "Stay where you are. I'll go find more water."

The boy knew how precious fresh water was. He knew it was a terrible waste to spill so much, but he couldn't help it. Because of the recent storms, however, Yamawe had plenty more rainwater collected in containers outside the *ba-ak*. In a few moments he returned with another, smaller jug. He let his nephew drink first and gather his strength, and then helped him get back on his feet. The boy was steadier after the brief rest.

Once again, Yamawe handed him the jug and said, "Now, go take this water to the stranger. He's waiting for you."

The boy managed to hold on to the jug this time instead of dropping it like a child. He was angry with his uncle, and that gave him added energy. He couldn't believe Yamawe was making him wait on the stranger.

When he entered the hut, a damp, putrid smell took his breath away. His aunt, Hamala, lay far to the left of the door flap, close to the wall. Her back was turned so he couldn't see her face, but he could hear her labored breathing. It came in short, quick gasps.

The stranger lay on the opposite side of the hut. When the boy's tired eyes adjusted to the dim light, he saw the man look at him. The stranger's eyes were sunken in his face. They looked glassy and he seemed to have a hard time keeping them open. His face was long and narrow, and no tattoos or piercing decorated his cheeks and lips. Instead, a dirty beard grew around his mouth and chin. He was bony and thin, but the boy didn't know if that was because of the man's long journey or because of the illness.

The sick sailor kept licking his lips. The boy could tell he was thirsty, but he just stood there and stared at him for a minute. He wasn't sure why, but he wanted to see what the stranger would do. Would he beg for the water? Would he demand it? Would he try to get up and take it? The angry boy didn't know exactly what he wanted from the sick man. He just wanted to hate the stranger, and he wanted the man to know it.

Finally, Yamawe came into the hut. He saw his nephew standing motionless and barked, "Nephew, give the man some water!" Reluctantly, the boy held out the jug toward the stranger.

"Here. Take it," he said, glaring at the man.

The sailor reached up with one hand, using the other to

support himself. He never took his dull eyes off the boy, who kept taunting him with the water jug, holding it just high enough that the sick man couldn't reach it.

Yamawe snatched the jug from his nephew's hands and knelt beside the stranger. Steadying the man so he could take a drink, Yamawe used hand signs to urge him to drink slowly.

Without turning to look at him, his uncle ordered, "Stay outside, Nephew. There is no space for you here if you won't be helpful."

The remark fed the boy's anger even more. He stormed from the hut and stopped by the fire pit outside, warming his hands and talking to his dog.

"It's all wrong," the boy muttered. "Uncle should be taking care of me first, not that stranger. I'm tired and weak and he's telling me to wait on that dirty man like he's a welcome guest!" He moved as close to the fire as he could. He was shivering.

"Maybe I'm getting sick again," he said as he rubbed his arms, trying to warm up. "Maybe I've brought the sickness to Uncle and he'll get it too. Then I'll ignore him the same way he's ignoring me and he'll know how it feels!"

But even as he said it, he knew he didn't mean it. Yamawe had saved him. He had brought him water and had offered him a place to stay. Yamawe hadn't caused the troubles; the strangers had. The boy did have to respect his uncle, but he didn't have to respect the stranger. And he didn't have to be happy about any of it.

Yamawe came outside and bent over the fire. He stirred the coals, breathing heavily from the effort. "I can't take care of all of you. I'm tired and hungry. You're going to have to help me, or stay out of the way."

"I don't mind helping you," the nephew answered. "I just don't want to help the stranger."

"If you want to help me, you will do as I tell you," Yamawe replied in a cold voice. "Now, we need food. Go check the fish traps. There should be plenty of fish; I haven't had a chance to check them in days."

Yamawe didn't move when he finished speaking. He remained squatting by the fire, warming his hands, and staring into the flames. The boy waited for a moment, but he could tell his uncle wasn't going to say anything more. And if he wanted to stay with Yamawe, he had to follow his orders.

Still, he hesitated for a minute. Did he really want to be treated like this? Didn't he deserve better care from his own relative? He knew if he didn't obey his uncle, though, he wouldn't be welcome to stay. And that left the orphaned boy with little choice. If he left in anger, he'd be on his own, and there was no way he could survive alone, weak and hungry. All he had left was his anger, and that wouldn't fill his empty stomach. Wearily, the boy stood up.

"It's getting dark. I'll check the nearest trap tonight and leave the others until morning," he said. He wondered how he would find the strength, but he said nothing more.

Without waiting for Yamawe to reply, the boy stumbled unsteadily toward the small inlet behind the dunes. If no fish were in the trap, maybe he could spear a few crabs for their supper. There were also roots they could roast and eat, but digging them was hard work and he was just too weak. He hoped for the best and headed to gather the fish from the cages.

The days that followed were much the same. Yamawe sent his nephew to gather fish or firewood, while he stayed at the *ba-ak*, tending the two sick ones. He and the boy didn't talk much. The boy didn't like the change in Yamawe. He had always been a fun-loving uncle, ready to stand up for his nephew when Behma seemed too strict. And Yamawe had always taken pride in his appearance, his strength and his skills as a hunter—as a provider for his new wife. Now he seemed hard and irritable, dirty and demanding.

Yamawe cooked the food the boy managed to gather each day, and they ate in silence around the outside fire. Yamawe never again asked his nephew to do anything for the stranger. Instead he took care of both his wife and the sailor while the boy stayed outside. The boy even slept outside. He was warm enough by the fire with his dog beside him. He didn't want to be anywhere near the stranger, and he couldn't stand the stench of sickness inside the hut. He felt cleaner and healthier in the fresh air, even if it was chilly and damp.

His stomach was still weak from the sickness and he couldn't eat very much at a time. That was just as well, since he wasn't able to gather very much food. Even so, he knew he was slowly getting stronger, little by little. At the same time, he could see his uncle growing weaker and weaker from taking care of both Hamala and the stranger.

"They are going to live," Yamawe told his nephew one morning, "but they are still far from well."

The boy just nodded in response.

"This means you'll need to bring more fish now, and begin digging roots. Those foods will sit easy on their stomachs and make them grow stronger," Yamawe said.

The boy felt mistreated and annoyed, but he bowed his head. What choice did he have? He knew that his own diet would suffer if he didn't go along with his uncle. If he didn't provide more food, Yamawe would simply divide the boy's meager share to feed the others, and the boy would end up hungrier and weaker. And Yamawe would still expect him to keep doing all the work.

Later that morning, when he plodded back to the *ba-ak* with the fish he'd found in the traps, the tired boy was shocked to see the stranger sitting by the outside fire. The man sat alone with his eyes closed and his head tipped back, his face soaking up the warmth of the midday sun. He was so thin that his ribs showed through his skin. His hair was long and matted, not braided or pulled back with a strip of deer hide like the Karankawa men wore theirs.

For a minute the boy forgot to be angry and allowed himself to sympathize with the man. He understood how much of a relief the fresh air and sunshine could be. Then the dog trotted up next to the sick sailor and licked his hand. Startled, the stranger pushed the dog away. He wasn't rough. He didn't push the dog any harder than the boy sometimes did himself. But that act dissolved the young Karankawa's sympathy and rekindled his anger.

"Hey!" he shouted.

The stranger turned slowly in the direction of the voice, with a questioning look.

"That's my dog. Leave him alone," the youngster said angrily, even though he knew the man couldn't understand.

The dog returned to his master's side and nipped at the basket of fish he held. "Go away!" he snapped at the pup. Without thinking, he pushed the animal away the same way the stranger had just done.

When he saw that, the stranger actually laughed. "Hey!"

he said again, as if they shared a joke.

The boy glared at him. The man kept smiling at him. The dog jumped around in circles with the most enthusiasm it had shown since the sickness. Finally, the boy decided to just ignore the stranger altogether and turned to toss the dog a fish. "Good dog. Now go away," he said sternly.

The basket was starting to get heavy, so he set it down. His uncle was nowhere to be seen.

"Uncle?" he called loudly. "Yamawe? I've brought the fish."

There was no answer. The stranger studied him. "*El hombre?*" he said in his own language this time. "*Está allá.*"

The Karankawa boy had no idea what the words meant, but the stranger pointed at the hut. Understanding his gesture, the boy glanced that direction and scowled. Why hadn't Yamawe answered?

The nephew peered through the door flap and was surprised to see his uncle lying next to his wife, Hamala. This time Yamawe was the one panting in pain. Hamala knelt beside him and rubbed a stone on his belly in slow circles. She glared at her nephew through sunken, bloodshot eyes. Her bottom lip was pierced with a thin piece of cane and it reminded him of his mother's similar jewelry. The blue tattoos on her cheeks looked faded against her sickly gray skin. The strands of her tree moss skirt lay tangled and dirty around her legs.

"The warm stone eases the stomach cramps. Bring me another that is heated by the fire when you bring my food and water," she ordered, her raspy voice barely above a whisper.

The nephew dropped the deer hide, stunned at the sudden change of events. Now his uncle lay sick, maybe dying, and his aunt had taken charge. Things had gone from bad to worse. Hamala was not an easy person to be around. She didn't get along with the other women in the village. She thought she was better than they were; they thought she was lazy and dirty. He had never understood why his uncle married her. Yamawe seemed blind to all her faults and deaf to her sharp tongue.

Dismayed, the nephew trudged back to the fire where the stranger looked up expectantly, as though he was waiting for a report on the situation. He had a confident manner about him. The boy wondered what kind of man he was and where he had come from. Did he usually have servants to wait on him? Did he lead warriors in battle? Was he a ruler, a chief?

The boy shook the questions from his mind. It was the fault of the stranger, he reminded himself, that he was stuck here at all. The stranger, no matter who he was, owed him a lot. He'd have to figure out how to make the man pay for the pain he'd brought, but first the boy needed to deal with the problems at hand: finding food and gathering strength. Getting revenge would have to wait.

Sitting down next to the basket of fish, the brooding youngster took a sharp oyster shell, slit each fish open and scooped out the guts. The stranger watched but made no move to help. When the fish were cleaned, the boy found the roasting sticks Yamawe had been using and threaded several fish onto each one. He handed one of the sticks to the stranger and kept two for himself. He held them over the fire, turning them slowly as the fish cooked. The sailor watched for a minute and then followed suit. His eyes met the boy's briefly, but then he turned his concentration to the task, watching intently as the fish skins sizzled and browned in the flames. After many long, silent minutes, he held up his roasting stick and raised one bushy eyebrow.

"Hey!" he said to get the boy's attention. He jerked his head to gesture at the fish he held.

The boy didn't answer right away. First he studied his own fish and decided they were done, and then he got up and checked the stranger's. "Good," he grunted.

He kicked a stone away from the fire. When it had cooled enough to handle, he picked it up. Then he delivered the stone along with some fish and water to his aunt, as she had ordered. When he returned to the fire, he was surprised to see that the stranger hadn't eaten any of the fish yet. He had expected the man to gorge himself. In fact, he had secretly hoped the sailor would do just that and make himself sick again from putting too much food into his empty stomach too soon. Instead, the man waited until the boy showed him, using signs, that the fish were indeed his to eat. Then the boy squatted near the fire to eat his own. The dog wandered up and nosed around for scraps.

The stranger ate quickly but carefully. He paused when only the first fish's head and tail were left. "Hey!" he called to the dog, tossing the pieces to him.

"Good," he said and then looked at the boy to see if he had used the right word. The Karankawa boy couldn't tell if the man really knew what the word meant, but it fit, so he nodded. The sailor seemed pleased with himself and mumbled, "good, good" to himself, as though practicing how to say it.

They sat in silence, eating and sharing the scraps with the dog. After some time, the stranger pointed at the boy. "Chico," he said. Then he pointed at himself. "Jefe."

He repeated the words several times. Each time he said "Chico" he pointed at the boy. And each time he said "Jefe" he pointed at himself. When he stopped, he looked at the boy and nodded encouragingly. The boy wasn't sure what the man wanted, but decided he wanted him to repeat the words.

As he pointed at himself and tried to say "Chico," the boy realized what the sailor was trying to tell him. The man wanted to call him "Chico," and the boy should call the man "Jefe." The Karankawa boy was relieved. This would help. No matter how much he disliked the stranger, they were going to have to communicate now that Yamawe was too sick to be the go-between.

"Chico. Jefe." the boy repeated, pointing. The man grinned and said both names again.

Then he pointed at the dog. "Good," he said, as if that were the dog's name. Chico laughed at him. Maybe Jefe, the stranger, wasn't all that smart after all.

In the end, though, Jefe proved he did have some intelligence. This was his first real food in a long time. The sailor must have been ravenous, but he stopped before eating too much. Maybe he'd had some experience with hunger. He seemed to know how important it was to ease his body back slowly. Chico was glad that Jefe had at least shown good sense about that. He was going to be much more useful healthy than sick, even though, deep down, Chico would have enjoyed the easy revenge.

That morning, before he got sick himself, Yamawe had ordered Chico to start gathering roots as well as fish.

Chico decided to spend the afternoon scouting for the plants. He planned to dig a few, but only enough to get by. He resented his uncle's demands, and he dreaded the strenuous work, but Chico had to admit the starchy roots sounded appetizing. His hunger just wasn't satisfied by a diet of fish alone. Roots roasted over hot coals would be a filling meal and a welcome change of pace.

He felt a pang, remembering how his mother always seasoned the roasted roots with wild garlic to cover their bitter taste. Waves of sadness flooded over him and his eyes grew misty. He missed his family so much.

Then, just as quickly, the sight of the stranger, Jefe, jolted him out of the memories and into the present. The sorrow evaporated and anger rushed back in.

Strengthened by that surge of anger, Chico promised himself again to survive, no matter what. If he had to live at his uncle's *ba-ak* with a stranger he hated, he'd do it until he could find a way out. He'd use the hate to keep himself going. He rose with new energy and cast a glare at Jefe, who couldn't understand the boy's sudden mood change. Then Chico whistled for his dog, and headed for the swampy marsh grasses.

He wanted to survive, and he wanted to get rid of Jefe the stranger. He needed some kind of plan.

Chapter 5

Until now, Chico had always waited for somebody else to figure things out, but that was going to have to change. Now there was nobody else. His uncle and aunt had turned their attentions to each other. The boy was nothing to them.

He tried to sort out his thoughts as he walked. He knew he was on his own. He knew he was young. He knew he didn't have much experience. He also knew that there was nothing left in the island village for him. He needed to find a place to live, a place where he could grow to be a man—a place where he belonged.

But first he wanted revenge.

He wanted to make the stranger pay for the pain he'd brought. Chico wanted him to see the hate he felt growing inside. The boy smiled to himself. He'd make him suffer. And he'd humiliate him.

First of all, he'd make the stranger work. Hard. He'd start tomorrow by giving Jefe the job of digging roots. Even in good health, it was an exhausting chore. Chico knew Jefe wasn't strong enough to do it. Plus, it was women's work. Men never stooped to such hard labor. Jefe would suffer, and Chico would enjoy causing the pain and humiliation.

Chico felt better already. Thoughts of revenge made him feel powerful.

It was quite a walk to the marshy area between the island and the mainland. He and the dog both stopped to rest on the last dry dune. Shading his eyes from the sun's glare, he studied the wide stretch of boggy water. The marsh water rose and fell with the tides, just as the seawater did on the sandy beach. A variety of shore birds stopped here to feast on the clams and crabs and small fish in the calm, shallow water. Swamp rabbits kept burrows here.

Small alligators hid among the thick reeds. Long-necked herons kept silent watch over the watery landscape.

And there were snakes.

Snakes were abundant both on the island and in the marsh. Some lived in the water, holding only their heads above water, their long bodies trailing unseen below the surface. Others slithered along the warm sand in the dunes, absorbing the heat to warm their bodies. In the winter, cool weather made the snakes sluggish and slow to react. If startled, though, they would still lash out with a hiss or a rattle and often a bite. Some had long fangs filled with poison that could kill a man. Such was an awful death; it began with swelling and tingling, then turned into burning pain.

Chico shuddered and pulled the dog close. Until that moment, he had forgotten about the snakes. He felt a rise of panic. He'd never been afraid out on the open sand, but suddenly he didn't want to wade into the marsh or put his hands under the dark, muddy water. Who knew what might be lurking there?

"Maybe it will be safer near the edge of the water," he thought hopefully.

Tomorrow, he reminded himself, he'd be sending Jefe into the swampy lagoon in his place, weak, exhausted, and careless. With luck, maybe Jefe would run into a snake.

Chico snapped out of his reverie. Today the job of finding food still fell on him. Yamawe had told him to gather roots, and Hamala would expect him to bring them food. For the moment he needed to stop daydreaming about tomorrow's revenge and take care of today's responsibilities.

He took a deep breath and stood up.

Trying to remember everything he had heard his mother teach his sister about digging roots, Chico waded at the edge of the brackish water. He probed ahead with the long, sharp digging stick. He hoped that any snakes hidden in the grasses would swim away from the disturbance. Chico shivered with relief to see nothing more than a few bugs fly up and some tiny water spiders skid across the water.

It didn't take long for him to choose a clump of reeds. He felt around under the water until he found a spiny bulb. Using his stick, he pried the bulb away from the mucky bottom, and then broke the bulb free from the long, stiff stalk. The roots themselves were spiny and the leaves on the reed were sharp as knives. Before long his fingers stung from many tiny pricks and his arms burned where the reeds scratched them. The shallow water in the marsh was cloudy, and it turned even murkier as he pulled up plants and stirred up the muddy bottom.

When the basket was only half full, he decided he'd

gathered enough. His back ached. His arms and hands throbbed. They were swollen and red. He cleaned the cuts in a tide puddle just outside the marsh. The still water there was clean and it helped a little to ease the pain, but he wished instead he could go for a swim in the soothing salt water on the seaside of the island.

The dog had spent the afternoon nearby, as always. Part of the time he nosed through the grasses up on the dunes. He pawed at an abandoned nest he discovered and chased a startled bug that flew up. But before long, he ran out of energy and simply sprawled on the sand. He didn't have all his strength back yet, either. Chico envied him the chance to lie in the sun and do nothing.

He pictured Jefe doing the same thing and gritted his teeth. "Not after today," Chico promised himself.

Balancing the basket of roots against his hip, he began the walk back to his uncle's home. Hours of wading in the chilly water and stooping to dig the roots had sapped much of his newfound energy. He stopped several times on the trip back to shift his load and stretch his cramping muscles. He was tired, but proud of himself. His strength was returning slowly, but he could tell that it truly was coming back at last. He felt sure now that he'd be able to make his own way.

When Chico finally got back to the hut, Jefe still sat by

the fire pit. A deer hide was draped around his shoulders. He dozed in the fading sunlight; his head drooped to his chest. The leathery skin sagged on his bony arms. But his breathing was deep and steady, proving that his body was no longer ravaged with the sickness. He was weak, but he was no longer sick.

Chico was pleased. Jefe could start carrying his own weight tomorrow.

The boy heaved the basket of roots to the ground by the fire with a loud grunt. He was trying to startle Jefe but was disappointed to get no reaction. Eventually, Jefe's droopy eyes opened. He lifted his head and looked directly at Chico.

"Hey!" he nodded at the boy in greeting, gesturing for him to join him at the fire.

Chico cast a stern look his direction and pretended he didn't understand. He began to empty the basket, examining each root before placing it onto the coals along the outside of the fire. He wasn't sure why he handled them so carefully. His mother had always done it this way so it never occurred to him to do it any differently. Cooking, like digging the roots, was women's work in a Karankawa village. Tomorrow, the women's jobs would go to Jefe.

And tomorrow, Chico decided, he would take on the

responsibilities of a man.

Hunting was a man's job. During the chilly winter, his father and the other men hunted for small animals that lived along the marshy lagoon, between the island and the mainland. They were excellent marksmen with their long cedar bows and their cane arrows. Chico remembered Behma's sturdy bow. It was as long as his father was tall, and always well polished with shark oil to keep the wood from cracking. That wonderful bow had burned with the rest of the hut. All Chico had now was Behma's fishing spear. He shrugged. He couldn't have used the bow anyway. The bowstring was strung so tight that only a very strong man could shoot with it.

"Someday," Chico muttered to himself. "Someday I'll have one of my own."

"Eh?" Jefe grunted, startling Chico from his thoughts. "*Qué dice?* Did you say something?"

Chico shook his head and finished his task, covering the roots with hot coals. He would leave them to roast all night. In the morning the charred skin would flake off and the bulbs would be pasty and soft. They had a slightly bitter flavor, but the starchy bulbs would make a filling meal.

Chico rose stiffly from his squatting position. He stretched his tired back and shoulders and flexed his tender hands.

"Tomorrow, Jefe, this becomes your job," he pointed from the basket to the fire to the Spaniard. He repeated his hand motions to be sure Jefe understood.

When the older man smiled, Chico just nodded solemnly and walked away. He checked on Yamawe and Hamala in the *ba-ak*. They were sleeping. He couldn't tell if his uncle was better or worse. He was just glad his aunt was well enough to take care of her husband and leave Chico alone.

His day's chores completed, Chico settled down by the fire. He was tired. Tomorrow, he reminded himself, he'd have the pleasure of making Jefe suffer. Sighing, he put his arm around his dog, and together they stayed warm as they drifted off to sleep.

—

The next morning, the sky was gray and a thick fog lay over the island. The sunlight was thin and watery. Chico shivered in the chilly damp. The fire's warmth felt so good that he hardly noticed the burning as he pulled the roasted roots from the embers. He placed enough inside the hut's flap for his aunt and uncle to eat when they woke, then he hurried back to the fireside. Jefe watched him scrape the burned skin from the roots and then did the same himself.

Before long, both were eating in silence.

"Come," Chico said when he finished eating.

He hoped he sounded commanding. He took up his father's fishing spear and handed the basket and the digging stick to Jefe. The dog led the way across the back of the island to the same swampy patch where Chico had dug roots the day before. Jefe stumbled a couple of times along the unfamiliar path, but he never cried out. Chico decided to test Jefe's stamina, and he began walking faster.

"Perfect!" Chico thought, breathing heavily himself. The air was thick with moisture. The mist made it difficult to see anything except what was right in front of him. Jefe would not only suffer from the chill and the damp, he'd also have to strain to see what he was doing and where he was going.

Chico and his dog continued down the path. Finally he paused at the base of the dune to let Jefe catch up. The tidal marsh stretched before them. Chico waved his arm to gesture across the whole expanse.

He pointed to the basket and signed what he wanted Jefe to do. He wanted the basket mounded over with roots. He had to repeat the motions several times before Jefe nodded that he understood.

"Now go!" Chico said sternly. "Work!"

"*Qué?*" Jefe looked confused. He shrugged his shoulders

and held his palms up questioningly.

Chico was irritated. He yanked the digging stick from Jefe's hand and splashed into the water. He jerked at the first plant he found, dug out the root, and broke it from its stem. The familiar spiny skin pricked his hands. He smiled grimly. Then he looked up at Jefe, shoved the root and the digging stick at him, and splashed back to the sand where his dog waited.

Chico didn't look back. Instead he deliberately walked out of sight into the dunes. He planned to spend the day hunting for other food among the dry dune grass. Even this time of year he might find bird eggs, small rabbits, or crabs. Maybe he'd find some fish trapped in a tide pool. At any rate, he refused to tackle the backbreaking job of gathering roots.

"Let the sailor suffer," he said to himself.

Chico returned from his hunt empty-handed several hours later. Jefe had left the marsh. The sun had emerged when the early morning clouds burned off and now it was shining brightly high overhead. Chico saw Jefe laying spread eagle on the sand, stretched out like a snake soaking up warmth on a sunny day.

He was furious to find Jefe resting.

Chico ran toward the man, shouting and waving his arms. Jefe sat up and studied his wild gesturing. Then he pointed at the basket. Chico stopped and stared. He couldn't believe his eyes. The basket was full to the brim with roots, mounded over at the top, just as he'd told Jefe to fill it.

Chico couldn't have been more disappointed. He'd wanted Jefe to suffer. He thought he had set him up to crush him. It was true the man looked fatigued from the labor, but not broken. And he had finished the job and done it correctly.

Angry that his plan to humiliate Jefe seemed to be failing, Chico jerked his finger at the basket and said sharply to Jefe, "Let's go." The he turned to take the path toward home.

"Chico?" Jefe called. He nodded helplessly at the basket, and held out the digging stick for Chico. He gestured that he couldn't carry both now that the basket was heavy and full. Chico snatched the digging stick and whistled for his dog.

Jefe followed behind. He breathed heavily and shifted the awkward load every few steps. Progress was slow. Chico took great satisfaction from Jefe's discomfort. He'd noticed that Jefe's hands were bloody and raw, and his arms and legs were covered with scratches from the sharp cane leaves.

The dog wandered beside the path, running between

Chico and Jefe. Although he stopped every few feet to sniff at scents left by creatures long gone, he never managed to track down anything. He made so much noise bumbling through the grass and sand and shells that most animals were startled and took off well ahead of him.

Chico kept a good pace for a while, but it wasn't long before he found himself panting. Not wanting to let Jefe know that he was tiring, he pretended he was pausing to let Jefe catch up. The boy waited, resting and glaring at the sailor trudging up the dune behind him.

"Hurry up!" Chico barked. When he was near enough, he reached out and prodded Jefe in the ribs with the sharp fishing spear.

Jefe looked up with a startled expression. He dropped the heavy basket and snatched the pointed stick from Chico's hand. Chico gasped and instinctively pulled back. In that moment, he realized he'd gone too far. He shouldn't have taunted him. Jefe may have been sick, but he was still a grown man, probably stronger in his weakness than Chico had ever been.

And then he saw Jefe aim the lance in the dog's direction.

Chapter 6

Fear and anger and helplessness shot through the boy. Before he could stop him, Chico watched Jefe lunge forward and throw the spear with one mighty thrust, just as the dog crossed the path in front of him.

"No!" the boy cried, sinking to his knees. He covered his face with his hands.

A yelp, then silence. A breeze blew; stiff dune grasses rattled.

Chico finally dared to raise his head. He saw Jefe hunched over with his hands on his knees, trying to catch his breath. Then he saw the dog dancing around Jefe, licking and nipping at him, before darting away to sniff at the fishing lance stuck upright in the sand. Chico didn't understand.

Jefe turned his head to look at Chico. He gave a tired grin. "*Serpiente,*" he said, bobbing his head toward where the stick stood. Chico stepped near. He couldn't believe his eyes.

The spear pinned a rattlesnake to the ground. Jefe had not been trying to attack Chico's dog—he had been trying to save him.

Chico remembered that Jefe had been paying close attention to the trail to keep from stumbling with the heavy basket. But when Chico prodded him with the sharp spear, Jefe had flinched and jerked his head up. In that instant he must have spied the snake at the side of the path.

Chico stared at the snake. It had probably been sunning itself in the warm sunshine when the dog disturbed it. Jefe stood up now with his hands on his waist, still trying to catch his breath. The dog sniffed cautiously at the dying snake's quivering tail. Roots, from the basket, lay scattered across the path.

Chico didn't know how to react. He didn't know what to do. Jefe had saved them. He was not the villain Chico had wanted him to be.

Chico squatted down and his dog scampered over and licked him in the face. The boy was glad to bury his face in the dog's sandy fur and hide the tears that stung his eyes. Finally, the dog pushed him off balance with his enthusiastic licking. Chico clung to him a moment longer, and then he struggled to his feet.

As he stood, he saw Jefe reach down to pull the lance's tip from the snake's neck. Without a second thought, Chico shoved him aside with a warning cry.

"Eh?" Jefe asked with a confused look. He staggered to regain his footing.

Chico picked up the digging stick and jabbed at the snake's triangular head. Immediately, the serpent's wide mouth opened and needle-like fangs sank into the wooden shaft.

The boy knew that even a dead rattlesnake was still dangerous. He knew that long after a snake had been killed, its muscles and reflexes would still react. And if a dead snake's fangs sank into a man's skin, the poison was just as deadly as when the snake was alive. Now that the venom had been released into the stick, the snake could do no more harm. Its power was completely gone and the danger was finally past.

Jefe shuddered. Chico saw him and laughed a little in shaky relief.

The relief wasn't just about killing the snake. He didn't understand why, but Chico somehow felt free of his anger and his need for revenge. He saw clearly now that Jefe had suffered as much as he had. Their problems were the same. They'd both lost everything because of the shipwreck and the sickness.

"Umph," Jefe grunted. He stooped to pick up the scattered roots, staying well out of range of the snake's body. Chico knelt to help him.

Jefe extended his hand. Chico reached out and clasped Jefe's arm firmly. Jefe nodded at Chico. Then they went back to work.

In short order, they loaded the scattered roots back into the basket. Chico pulled the spear from the ground; the snake still dangled from the weapon's sharp point. The dog trotted beside them as they slowly made their way back to the uncle's *ba-ak.*

At the fire pit, they set to work immediately. Chico used a sharp shell knife to skin the rattlesnake. First he removed the head. He took a last look at the beady eyes and hideous fangs and tossed it into the fire with a shiver. Next he cut off the tail with its rattles and set that piece aside. Finally he made one long slice down the belly from neck to tail, scraped out the entrails and carefully peeled the skin away from the meat. He spread the skin out to dry. He cut the meat into pieces and threaded it onto roasting sticks.

Jefe sorted the roots and arranged them in the coals. He handled them gingerly.

"Your hands? *Etsma?*" Chico asked, holding his own up and wiggling his fingers.

Jefe stretched open his tender palms and held them out. "*Manos*," he said.

Chico winced when he saw Jefe's scratches and raw fingertips. He understood how sore they must be. His own hands still ached from yesterday's work, and he'd found it hard to even hold the knife tight enough to skin the snake.

After adding driftwood to the fire, he stirred the coals to make it blaze. The snake meat sizzled. He was too tired to hike down to the beach for salt water, so he poured a small amount of precious fresh water into a shallow pottery bowl

"For your *manos*," Chico set the round-bottomed bowl in front of Jefe. He splashed his own sore hands in the water to show Jefe what to do. Then he disappeared into the *ba-ak*.

Chico emerged from the hut a moment later. He

carried a small container to the fireside where Jefe sat soaking his hands. The boy dipped two fingers into the container and smeared something greasy and smelly on his hands. Then he offered the pot to Jefe, who wrinkled his nose. Chico insisted, so Jefe dipped out a small amount of the rancid alligator oil. It smelled spoiled, but Chico knew it would soothe their raw skin.

"*Bueno*," Jefe nodded. "*Gracias*. Good. Thank you."

Chico picked up the rattlesnake tail and shook it. Jefe laughed. Then Chico motioned for him to turn around and he began to braid Jefe's tangled hair. Even though it reached his shoulders, it wasn't as long as most Karankawa men wore their hair. Chico separated the snarls with his fingers, working the hair into a single braid. He finished by tying the rattles at the end.

When Jefe shook his head, they heard a muted rattle.

"It is Karankawa tradition to wear a snake's rattle," Chico said. "*Kumna*? Do you understand?" He tried to explain. "It shows the world your bravery. And now that we've killed the snake, we'll eat it. Not only will it give us strength, it means we have destroyed its spirit forever."

Chico pointed to the hot meat. He handed Jefe one of the roasting sticks and took one for himself. Then he pulled off a chunk of meat, blew on it, and put it in his mouth. Chewing slowly, he gestured for Jefe to do the same.

Jefe hesitated. Chico waved his hand in encouragement. "It's good. It will make you stronger." He flexed an arm and pointed to his muscle to illustrate his meaning. Then he licked his fingers and reached for another piece of the meat.

Jefe hesitated, and then he tore a chunk of meat from his stick and swallowed it in one quick motion. Chico watched his expression to see what he'd do next. Jefe took a second chunk. This time he chewed slowly.

Jefe licked his lips. "*Bueno.* Good."

"*Bueno. Pla,*" Chico repeated, pleased that they were beginning to understand each other. Jefe held up a piece of meat and called to the dog. Without hesitating the dog snatched the morsel. He sat, quivering, begging for more, but the men finished the rest of the meat themselves. It was a dense, stringy meat, more filling and satisfying than fish. And it was a welcome change from the fish they'd been eating for days.

The hut flap rustled. The men turned when they heard a sharp whistle. Chico's aunt put her head outside.

"Bring me that food, boy!" Hamala shouted. "Why should you eat before I do?"

She demanded fish as well as roots. Chico tried to explain that the fish traps had all been empty. He'd not been able to catch any small game; his hunting skills were poor and he had no bow. He didn't mention the snake.

"No excuses!" his aunt screeched. She shook her fist, "Bring something now!" Then she snapped the flap closed.

Chico took her some of the roots that had just started roasting. He knew they'd be crunchy and bitter, but it was all he had to give her. He was glad that he and Jefe had already eaten the rattlesnake meat before she'd had a chance to snatch it away.

"This is worthless!" Hamala croaked, yanking the bowl from him and cuffing him on the ear. "My husband needs better food than this to get his strength back. From now on, we eat first and we eat the best food. Kumna? Do you understand?" Her voice dropped to a growl. "You and the stranger can eat grass for all I care. But you will bring meat for Yamawe and me."

Chico knew that Hamala was short-tempered, but the illness seemed to have made her completely unreasonable. Her demands and harsh words made the hair rise on his neck. Chico had desired to leave his uncle before–had imagined it many times. Now, he wished that he and Jefe could leave together.

In spite of difficult thoughts, Chico smiled to himself. At least they had eaten well tonight.

—

By the next week, Chico's uncle had recovered enough to come out of the *ba-ak* and sit outside by the fire.

"There is not enough food here," he announced. "It's time to move to the mainland."

Chico was happy to go. It would be a relief to get away from the bad memories. There would also be more food. The weather was too unpredictable on the island at this season and food was hard to find. The fish had left the shallow inlets and gone out into the deep waters to spawn.

Chico and Jefe wouldn't get away from digging roots, though. There were plenty of the plants it seemed, even on the mainland. But there would also be lots of oysters in the bay. Spring would come, and there would be bird's eggs. Blackberries would ripen.

Even though it was usually women's work, Chico and Jefe prepared for the move. Under Hamala's shrill direction, they rolled up the *ba-ak* and loaded all the possessions into the dugout canoe. She watched with her hands on her hips and found fault with everything they did. Yamawe, too, scowled at Chico. Beads of sweat stood on Yamawe's brow. His body was gaining strength, but he was far from well. The exertion of preparing for the move made him cross and quiet. Hamala's yammering made

Chico's head hurt. He couldn't imagine how it affected his weak uncle.

"Lazy fools!" Hamala complained to her husband, pointing at Chico and Jefe. "They did nothing while you lay sick. We all would have starved to death if I hadn't gathered roots myself," she lied. Her eyes narrowed and she tossed her head.

"Gathered roots yourself?" gasped Chico. He had meant to keep his tongue, but the statement was outrageous, even for Hamala.

"Nephew!" Yamawe scolded. It startled Chico. His uncle continued "I expected you to be more grateful after I rescued you. You and the stranger owe us your lives in exchange for all the care your aunt tells me she has given you. Your lives, do you hear me?"

"But she's mistaken. I..." Chico began to protest.

His uncle's hand flew with such speed that Chico lost his balance. Chico had not seen Yamawe move so quickly since the illness began. The wrestler's arm flew wildly out, in a slap that sat Chico down hard in the sand. Yamawe, too, staggered.

Chico looked up at his uncle. Their eyes met, and for a silent moment it seemed that Yamawe thought of what he had done. His hand was still open–still poised from the blow. Things had been difficult between Chico and his uncle since the illness came. Yamawe had been cold and demanding. Chico had been stubborn and resentful. Now, in this moment, as Chico sat in the sand and Yamawe stood unsteadily over him, uncle and nephew came to a crossroads. It was a moment that made Chico's heart stop. Then Yamawe spoke, and Chico knew his uncle had chosen a path.

"After making my ill wife gather food for lazy children, don't you dare lift your voice against me." said Yamawe. His voice was quiet and terrifying. His breath came in ragged gasps. Sweat rolled from his forehead. "You will work. I will work you to the bone for risking Hamala's health with your idleness." Then Yamawe turned away and staggered to the canoe.

Yamawe was still too weak to have seriously injured Chico. Still, the side of Chico's face smarted, and his arms trembled as he pushed himself back to his feet.

Jefe, who had watched in silence, stepped quickly to Chico's side. He took Chico's arm, as if to help steady him. Yamawe turned, looked on the Spaniard and the boy, and grunted. Then he turned away again. Chico saw Jefe clench his jaw. Chico caught his eye and shook his head slightly.

There had been a time when Chico would have called such words from Yamawe a playful joke. Chico might even have forgiven a slap delivered in a moment of frustration. The silence after the blow, however, was unmistakable. In an instant, Yamawe, the wrestler with the ready smile–the tease who could always cajole Chico back into good humor–had turned forever toward his wife and against his nephew. And in that moment, Chico too made a choice. After all, today Hamala lied about gathering roots, and Yamawe raised his hand against his nephew. What would tomorrow bring? Chico knew that Yamawe would never doubt his wife's word. The boy's heart was heavy. Yamawe had told him from the beginning, and now Chico knew: there was nothing for him here. The boy would no more daydream of leaving. He would leave. It was just a matter of time.

Once their few possessions were packed, the group climbed silently into the canoe. The dog jumped in as Chico pushed the boat into the shallow marsh.

"Not that filthy dog!" Hamala declared, pushing it roughly from the boat. The dog splashed next to the canoe. It pawed frantically, trying to climb over the side.

Without a word, Jefe reached out, picked up the wet dog by the neck, and placed it beside him in the boat. The dog stood awkwardly and shook, rocking the boat and spraying muddy water everywhere. Then, calmer, it gained its balance and sat at the sailor's feet. Jefe's eyes met

Hamala's, as if daring her to push the dog out again.

"Bah!" she shrugged. "I guess I can always use it in a stew if you don't start bringing us more food," the aunt threatened. She sat back with her arms crossed.

Using long poles, Jefe and Chico pushed the boat across the water, dodging the clumps of rushes that sat like islands in the lagoon. The marsh was just starting to wake up with the early spring weather. Many of the animals, especially the alligators and turtles, were sluggish and slow in the chilly water. The air was cool, but the sunshine was beginning to have a welcome warming effect.

For the next few weeks on the mainland, Chico and Jefe gathered nothing but oysters and roots. As the plants began to grow with the warm weather, though, the roots became more and more bitter. They took them to Hamala until even she couldn't stand the taste any longer. Then they moved down the coast where the blackberries were ripe.

As her own strength returned, Chico's aunt took over the job of cooking again, but only so she could control how much food Chico and Jefe got. She prepared the food on the fire inside the hut and gave them just enough to survive. Some days she gave them nothing at all. They were always hungry. The hard work, the changing weather, and the lack of sufficient food kept Jefe from getting his full strength back as quickly as Chico hoped. He didn't stop working, though, and he didn't complain. Yamawe did not strike his nephew again. Nor did he speak to him.

Chico and Jefe continued to sleep outside with the dog close beside them. The fresh air felt much better than the poisoned atmosphere inside the hut. At night they sat under the stars and used sign language to communicate with each other and make plans. With time they each learned words in the other's language, but often they managed well with only hand signals and gestures.

One night, Jefe asked Chico, "When shall we leave?" He waved his hand toward the forests on the far horizon.

Chico squinted at him. "Are you strong enough to go?" He reached over and squeezed the muscle in Jefe's upper arm. He got his answer. It was solid. Jefe was thin, but he had hard muscles on his bony frame.

"It doesn't matter to me when or where we go," Chico said, "as long as it's away from here. There is nothing left for me here, just as there is nothing left for you."

A group of sea gulls flew overhead. They squawked on their way to the open water.

"When I left my home far across the ocean, my ship was sailing to Pánuco, a Spanish outpost somewhere down the coast from here," Jefe said, stirring the fire and watching the sparks fly up toward the passing gulls. "We were coming to claim new lands for our king, the King of Spain. But between storms and bad judgment, we lost our way and finally shipwrecked on your island."

Chico scratched the dog's head and tried to understand Jefe's story.

"I don't know what you call your island." Said Jefe. "I call it *Malhado*, the Isle of Misfortune." He was silent for a moment, and then continued. "So many were lost at sea. And so many more died with the stomach sickness. Maybe some of my people survived, as I did. Maybe they are living in other villages, unable to leave or unsure where to go. I need to find them. I belong with them."

Chico wasn't sure he understood all that Jefe had said, but he didn't really care. In the end, all that really mattered to him was that they both wanted to leave.

Jefe told Chico about an idea he had. He explained his plan to travel from village to village, trading goods.

"We'll start by going to the people who live among the trees far beyond our camp here," he gestured to the forest in the distance. "Hamala will be happy to have two fewer mouths to feed!" he laughed. "Then we'll make our way from village to village, looking for my people, and trading as we go. Perhaps you can find friends or relatives who are kinder than your aunt and uncle. And somehow I'll find my way to Pánuco on the coast. There's a Spanish settlement there where I will be safe."

They planned and discussed their escape for many nights. They knew they needed to leave soon, before Yamawe was stronger and able to force them to stay. Planning carefully, they collected shells and pearls for trading. They sharpened the fishing spear and clam shell knife.

And finally, at the new moon, when the night was darkest, Jefe put a hand on Chico's thin shoulder. "We leave tonight."

Chapter 7

They picked their way quietly across the brushy coast toward the trees where the *Charruco*, the forest people, lived.

The night was dark and still. Chico's heart pounded with every snapped twig or scuffled shell. He was sure Yamawe would hear the dog scrambling through the scrub brush as they left the camp. If he demanded they come back, Chico knew he'd have to obey, even if Jefe could still get away. And then he'd be trapped. Going with Jefe was his only chance to escape a hard life with his shrewish aunt and resentful uncle.

"There's nothing left for you here," he remembered Yamawe telling him after his family died. At the time, Chico hadn't completely understood what that meant. Now he felt no sadness leaving the only home he'd ever known. There truly was nothing left for him. He didn't even look back. There was nothing to see; there were only memories. And those he carried inside.

A voice screeched behind them. Chico gasped, afraid it was his aunt calling after them. Jefe paused. "Shh," he motioned.

Another cry followed, and another. Chico let out his breath. It was only the gulls. Their voices were eerily human.

At dawn, the travelers came upon a scattered group of dirty huts. Smoke floated above a filthy *ba-ak* where a skinny man stood outside. He swayed unsteadily and puffed on a hollow clay pipe. He seemed startled to see them, but grinned menacingly when he saw the dog nosing around a pile of broken shells and discarded bones. Chico noticed the man's teeth were brown and uneven in his wide mouth. He'd never seen rotten teeth before. The island people had strong white teeth.

The man turned to Jefe and pointed at the dog.

"Yours?" he asked, raising an eyebrow on his broad forehead.

Jefe turned to Chico to translate. "Mine," Chico answered. He hoped his voice sounded firm enough to convince this awful looking man. He whistled and the dog came to stand safely next to him.

The man studied Jefe, the stranger. "Who is this?" he demanded.

Again, Jefe expected Chico to do the talking. "He is one of the sailors who washed up on the island after a shipwreck. Most of the others died of the stomach sickness. He goes now to look for a settlement of his own people."

"He brought the stomach sickness that killed so many of our people?" the man asked, growling. He puffed on the pipe and glared at Jefe. "He brought death. He must be a very evil man."

They stood in silence. The man's watery eyes brightened suddenly. "Why don't we get rid of him? We can just kill him," he suggested, "and then eat him." He snickered, giving Chico a sinister stare.

Chico's stomach turned over. Eat other people? He'd heard of savages who did such things. He'd been taught it was the most horrible act imaginable. To eat another person's flesh condemned his soul to never-ending torment. They needed to get away from this place as quickly as possible. If the man thought nothing of killing and eating Jefe, then he'd not think twice about killing the dog for a meal.

He stepped between Jefe and the dirty native. Behind his back Chico motioned for Jefe to back away. "It's wrong to think that this man killed our people. If he had such power, he wouldn't have allowed so many of his own to die. He's only one man. He's doing no harm. Go back to your pipe and we will go back to our journey."

Chico turned, snapped his fingers for the dog, and pushed Jefe ahead of him. "Go!" he said under his breath. Jefe heard the urgent tone and hurried into the thicket ahead.

Chico glanced back once when he felt something fly past his shoulder. The man still stood beside his dirty *ba-ak*. His pipe dangled from his rotten teeth as he scooped up mud balls and threw them at their backs. One dirt clod hit the dog's hind leg. He yelped and scurried ahead under a bush to lick the bruise.

Once they were finally out of sight, Chico and Jefe slowed down, but they didn't stop until the sun was high above them. Then they dropped wearily to the ground under a small tree. The brushy undergrowth was giving way to grass and bigger trees. For the first time since sneaking away from Yamawe's *ba-ak*, they relaxed, sure now that nobody had followed them.

"We've done it!" Chico grinned as he lay back to catch his breath.

He was excited. They'd escaped his aunt's abuse. They'd left behind the sorrow of the empty village. They'd made their way past the threatening savage. They'd survived. They were free to find their own way.

It was mid afternoon several days later when Chico and Jefe reached the Charruco, the people who lived among the trees. A large gray dog ran toward them, barking at Chico's dog. The two animals approached each other, circling and barking, nipping and sniffing. They wrestled briefly in the sandy dirt, and then ran off together like young boys playing.

Chico noticed with relief that the many dogs in the village appeared to be well fed and friendly. At least he didn't need to worry about his dog ending up in a stew that night.

The village, he saw, was just a small band of families, much the same as the group he'd grown up with. Four young girls worked side by side, scraping meat and hair from animal hides stretched out on the ground. When they heard the dogs barking, the girls looked up and stopped their work to stare at Chico and Jefe.

Chico heard their giggles and saw the girls wrinkle their noses. Last night he and Jefe had been plagued by mosquitoes and had smeared the last of Hamala's smelly alligator grease all over their bodies to protect themselves from the bites. The girls' reaction didn't bother him. He'd gotten used to the odor and was glad it had driven the mosquitoes away.

A man approached Chico and Jefe. His arms were open with welcome.

"You must speak for us," Jefe instructed Chico. "I don't know their language."

Chico looked nervous. "They are not my people. They may speak a different language, but I'll try. What do I say?"

Jefe gestured, and Chico did his best to interpret the meaning.

"We come from the coast with goods to trade. *Kumna*? Do you understand?" He began.

The Charruco man nodded. Relieved that their languages were similar, Chico continued. "We bring snail and conch shells for knives. We have beads and pearls."

The Charruco leader was delighted. "I am Halba. Please come eat at our fires. We will bring you food and then see what we can trade for your goods."

The villagers fed the traders and treated them well.

They even welcomed Chico's dog at the fire with their own dogs, tossing them scraps and bones. The food was different than Chico was used to, but he liked the new flavors. Instead of fish and roots, there was rich, red deer meat. The people shared willingly and made sure that Chico and Jefe ate until they were full.

Chico didn't know how to act among these new people. He watched Jefe and tried to copy his quiet dignity. The girls who had been scraping the hides now served the men their food. It felt strange to be treated equally with the men. He wasn't sure he belonged there. Halba, the leader, easily accepted him as a translator, though. Chico was proud to do it, but he was unsure he could handle such an important job. He'd never had adults depend on him in a man's role before.

He paid close attention to what Halba was saying.

The villagers were hunters. The man explained that they spent the winter in the shelter of the woods. When the weather allowed it, they trapped game, mostly deer, but also small bears and wild turkeys. They saved the deer hides and bearskins. They dried any extra meat to use when food was scarce. At times they traveled two or three days out to better hunting areas, but then they returned to their base camp where there was plenty of firewood and water. With the coming warm weather, they planned to go to the open prairies to hunt the bison grazing there.

"We hear there are even greater herds of these bison in the plains to the north, but we don't need to travel that far. Enough of them come to our prairies. We kill only what we can use," the leader told them.

Chico tried his best to translate to Jefe and hoped he got the correct meaning.

"We can offer you hides of deer and bison," Halba bargained, pointing to the animal skins stacked beside a nearby hut.

Jefe showed the people the shells and beads they had brought to trade.

"Red paint?" he asked, motioning as if his fingers were painting his face. "Flint?" he touched an arrow tip.

The leader nodded. He said something to a young boy who went immediately to one of the huts. Then he turned to Chico.

"It's good that you bring these things to trade. We need more hunting bows. The tribe across the prairie makes excellent bows from the wood of a special tree that grows where they live. We cannot trade with them because they are our enemies. You can go freely between us. If you will trade with them for us, you will always be welcome in our camps."

Chico used sign language and tried different words to talk more with Halba. He wanted to be sure he understood him correctly.

Jefe waited silently while the two talked. He nodded when Chico finally explained to him what the leader had proposed. "This is a good plan, Chico," he said. He sounded pleased. "It gives us the freedom to go wherever we want. They'll treat us well at all the villages and give us food because they know we will bring them the goods they need. And most importantly," he added, "we will have the chance to explore the land and find our way forward."

And that is exactly what happened.

They found the tribe across the prairie and traded shells and flint for their fine bows. Jefe insisted Chico keep one for himself, and then he taught him how to use it. At another village Chico traded his father's fishing spear for arrows. The spear was heavy to carry, and he didn't need it anymore. On top of that, it was a constant reminder of a life that no longer belonged to him. The bow was more useful anyway, although most often they traded for food instead of hunting it themselves.

In the seasons that followed, Chico and Jefe crossed the countryside, going from village to village. The people were glad to see them because the traders brought things they needed. Chico and Jefe lived with them, sat by their fires, ate their foods, and learned their different ways. Some ate their food raw; others cooked their food. Some had plenty to eat; others went hungry for days. Some smoked leaves that gave them visions; others drank special drinks that gave them strength. Some held celebrations with unfamiliar music and dancing. Some covered their bodies with tattoos; others wore animal skins.

At each stop, Chico learned words in new languages. Because they were traders, they were treated as welcome guests. Guests–but outsiders. They were welcome, it was true, but they didn't actually belong.

Jefe had Chico ask at every village about other sailors who might have survived the shipwreck and the sickness. And each time, Chico dreaded hearing the answer. Jefe and the dog were the only companions he had. They belonged together because they didn't belong anywhere else. But if Jefe found others of his own people, Chico was afraid he'd be left alone again.

If Jefe grew discouraged as the months passed with no news of other survivors, he never spoke of his worries. And Chico also kept his feelings to himself, embarrassed by his own fears. The two continued working side by side, concentrating on surviving from day to day.

—

The dog's barking woke Chico. In the distance, he saw a small group of Indians coming from the far side of the wide inlet where he and Jefe had camped near the coast. One of them appeared to be limping.

"Look," the boy pointed. Jefe grunted irritably. Chico shrugged off Jefe's bad mood and walked down the slope to greet them. Jefe stood at the top of the rise to watch.

After talking briefly with the visitors, Chico ran back to him, excited. "These men say there are three other Spaniards like you farther ahead!"

Jefe's eyes brightened. He slapped Chico on the shoulder and hurried past him to meet the men who were just reaching the camp. He took charge immediately and held his arms out in welcome, gesturing for them to sit at the fire. The dog ran from Chico to Jefe, barking with excitement. Chico tossed him a bone to make him stop annoying the visitors.

Jefe brought out a jug of water to share, and offered the men some of the dried meat they'd been given at the last village. The visitors passed around a ceramic pipe filled with sweet-burning leaves. One of them crossed his legs to prop his foot on the opposite knee. He winced as he brushed off the dirt.

"I noticed you were limping. What's wrong?" Chico asked.

"Yesterday I stepped on a fallen mesquite branch and one of the thorns stuck in the side of my foot. I pulled it out but now that part of my foot is puffy and sore. The skin is hot and it hurts to touch it," the Indian explained.

Chico knew how quickly cuts and scratches could fester. He'd had his share of them as a younger boy exploring the island and the marsh. He rose, tossed a couple of stones into the fire and picked up a shallow cooking pot. "Please excuse me. I'll be right back," he said.

He ran down the slope to the shore of the inlet and scooped up some of the salty water. When he got back to the campsite, he took the hot stones from the fire and dropped them into the pot to heat the water. Then when the bubbles stopped rising from the warm stones, he turned to the man with the hurt foot.

"Soak your foot until the water is cool. The warmth and the saltwater will draw out the pain and poison. Afterwards, squeeze the pulp from this leaf and rub the juice on the cut. The juice will help your foot heal," Chico said. He handed him the long, thick leaf of an aloe vera cactus.

The man followed Chico's instructions and slipped his foot into the nearly boiling water. As the pain began to diminish, his face relaxed with relief. "Thank you, young man. I'm in your debt."

"It's nothing," Chico objected. "My mother used warm saltwater for all kinds of ailments, and they told us about the healing plant at one of the villages where we stopped to trade. I'm just glad I could help you."

Jefe had waited patiently, but he was anxious to hear more news of his men. "Do they know the names of the men they saw?" Jefe asked Chico. The boy spoke to the Indians.

"There are two fair-skinned men, called Dorantes and Castillo, and there is a dark-skinned slave, called Estevanico," the Indians told him. "There were others, but the rest died of cold and hunger or were killed by other tribes."

Jefe shook his head in amazement. "I had almost lost hope," he declared. He slapped his leg in triumph. "Some of my men are still alive! Ask if they are well and where we can find them. Hurry!"

Chico asked the visitors for the information.

They said that Jefe's men were in a very sorry condition. They told Chico that Jefe's men were living among a tribe that kept them captive and beat them. They also told Chico that in two days, that tribe would gather nuts at a place nearby on the river's shore. Chico and Jefe might be able to meet them.

Jefe was ready to leave to find his shipmates right away, but Chico disagreed with that plan. "If this group of Indians has treated your men badly, why would they treat us any differently?" he asked. "We're strangers to them. Even though we are traders, it could be dangerous for us to go into this village. I don't like the way this sounds," he said with conviction.

Jefe paused. Chico didn't usually say so much. The older man scratched at his bearded face and nodded his head seriously. The rattlesnake rattles clattered in his hair. "It's true. We don't know anything about this tribe. We're farther south than we've ever traveled and we don't know the habits of the people here."

Jefe sighed. "But I've looked for so long," he said, staring across the water. "I can't pass up the chance to find any survivors. They don't belong here, used as slaves by those dirty natives. They're still my men," he announced in a firm voice. "They belong with me."

Chico held his breath. What he feared would happen was beginning to unfold.

"But what about me? I'm a dirty native. Where do I belong?" Chico muttered, afraid to know the answer.

Jefe heard the quiet question. He put his hand on Chico's shoulder and was startled to notice how much the boy had grown. He looked him in the eye now, as one man to another.

"You and I need each other," he said simply. "We belong together."

Chapter 8

Chico let out a sigh of relief, but he was still nervous.

"What if they would make us slaves?" he insisted.

"We'll be careful," Jefe assured him, "but we have to go and see for ourselves if what these men have told us is true. We'll take a long route to the river so we can watch out for any trouble."

The traveling Indians rested at the campsite with Chico and Jefe before continuing up the coast the next day. The injured man walked without pain after Chico's treatment. He took several aloe vera leaves with him in case they couldn't find any of the plants along their way.

Jefe and Chico spent two days making their way to the river. They had to go around the edge of the deep inlet at the coast, and then travel through rocky brush. As they neared the river, they came upon many trees heavy with nuts.

Crows perched high in the trees and flapped down to feast on fallen nuts in the shade of the branches. The birds were so intent on eating that they weren't disturbed by Chico and Jefe's presence. But when the dog ran at them, barking, they finally cawed and flapped off on lazy wings.

Meanwhile, brown squirrels scampered around the trees, gathering nuts that the crows hadn't yet reached. The dog ran from one tree to another, chasing the squirrels and trying without success to jump up and catch one. He made a huge racket and never seemed to get discouraged.

Chico and Jefe set up their camp in the dim coolness of the shady river bottom. Chico wandered down to the riverbank and peered into the placid flowing water. Small fish swam in quiet pools near the edge, nibbling at smooth, moss-covered rocks. Further downstream, the water foamed over short, rocky falls where the river changed levels. Then a sharp bend in the river changed the water's current so rapids bubbled through the narrow passage.

The dog's barking, the crows' screeching, and the squirrels' scolding chatter were the only things that broke the peacefulness of the place. It was a pleasant camp–or would have been if the dog had ever settled down.

Chico saw the other boy first. He had waded across a shallow section of water and was slinking along the riverbank, eyeing the barking dog.

"Hey!" Chico shouted and waved his arms. He ran toward the boy. "What are you doing?"

The dog bounded to Chico's side when he saw him running. The other boy stopped and held up his hands. Chico saw, as he got closer, that he was blind in one eye. His right eyeball was pale and seemed to have a thick film over it. It made the boy look strange, almost ghostly.

"Is that your dog?" he asked Chico in a different language than the Indians used near the coast. He tilted his head slightly to see better–out of his good eye. Chico recognized a couple of the words he used and generally understood what the boy asked.

"Yes, it is," Chico answered, resting a protective hand on the dog's head. He wondered what he wanted.

The other boy grinned. He reached out to let the dog sniff his hand, and then scratched him under the chin. Chico relaxed. The one-eyed boy was no threat. He was just another kid who liked dogs.

"I'm supposed to be picking nuts," the boy admitted. "But I heard the dog and wanted to find him. I didn't know there were more tribes on this side of the river."

"No other tribes," Chico said. "It's just me and another man. We don't belong anywhere in particular. We're traders and we travel from village to village. As we go, he looks for other sailors from his ship that wrecked on our island many, many months ago."

The boy paused petting the dog. He cocked his head to look at Chico. "Sailors? From across the ocean?"

"Yes, do you know of any?" Chico asked.

"Sure. There are three of them with the tribes that have come to pick nuts," the boy said. "Two are fair and have blue eyes. The third is big with much darker skin. He seems to be the smartest and friendliest. He tries to talk to me and has learned some of our language."

"Where can we meet them?" Chico discovered he was excited. He couldn't wait to tell Jefe.

"It would be too dangerous for you to come into our camp," the other boy replied. "Even though you're traders, your friend would be recognized as one of the sailors. Some of the people would try to hold him and use him for slave labor the same way they use the others."

Chico wanted to be sure he understood what the boy was saying. He held his palms up and shrugged to show he was unsure of his meaning.

"It's not good to be different." The boy tried to explain, using simpler words. "That's why they treat the strangers so badly. Some of them even kick and slap me, just because of my bad eye. Your friend is different too, with his pale skin and blue eyes. He should not go to the village, even as a trader."

Chico understood then what the boy meant. It was exactly what he had suspected. It wouldn't be safe. He was disappointed, though, because he knew Jefe would be disappointed. They were so close to Jefe's men, but how could they ever reach them?

"If he can wait, I might be able to help," the boy added.

He told Chico that the people would finish gathering nuts soon. Then they'd leave the river to move farther inland to the prickly pear grounds. The cactus fruit was nearly ripe, and many different tribes would be coming together to gather the fruit they called *tunas*. They would spend the next three moons picking the tunas.

The little purple fruits were juicy and sweet. They peeled them and ate them whole. They squeezed them and drank the juice. They dried them. They ground them into powder. They ate them until their bellies ached. And they danced and celebrated during the whole season. It was their happiest time of year because there was plenty to eat.

The sailors might be able to sneak away in the confusion because the Indians would be too busy to notice or care that they were gone.

The boy promised to take a message to Estevanico, the darker-skinned sailor. Meanwhile, he said, Chico and Jefe should make their way to the prickly pear fields. They should make their camp out of sight at the edge of the grounds and wait. By the time of the autumn full moon, he would send the sailors to meet them. With luck and good timing, they might be able to escape.

"Whatever you do, though," he told Chico before they parted, "when you leave here, don't go down the coast. The tribes there are cruel and already killed other sailors who washed up on their beaches. And when you and the other sailors make your escape, be sure to travel away from the prickly pear fields quickly and go inland where the people are friendlier."

They heard a shout and a whistle from the distance. The boy's mother had discovered he was missing and was calling for him in an angry voice. He squatted down and hugged the dog to himself.

"You're lucky," he told Chico. Then he slipped away through the trees, back down the river to his own village.

Chico shook his head. Lucky? That didn't make any sense. He must not have understood what the boy said.

—

Jefe and Chico made their way inland toward the prickly pears and camped far back in a thicket beyond the fields. As the weeks passed, tribes gathered from all directions. Dozens of people moved among the cactus, picking the spiny fruit. Children carried baskets. A few skinny dogs wandered from fire to fire, looking for a bit of food to snatch. And every night there was music and dancing and feasting.

Around the edge of the camp, the Indians built great bonfires of wet and rotten wood. The older men shouted at young boys to keep the smoky fires burning to drive away the clouds of mosquitoes. When the smoke blew toward the thicket, Chico's eyes watered. It was hard to sleep. The mosquitoes bit them all night, despite the smoke, and Chico wished he still had some of his aunt's alligator grease.

"Look!" Chico called quietly to Jefe after they'd waited and watched for several weeks. He rubbed his watery eyes. "I think that's the boy I talked to on the river." He pointed to his one-eyed friend who was busy adding wood to the fires.

"How will he know we're here?" Jefe wondered out loud.

"Let me try something," Chico said. "I have an idea

that might work."

He tossed a stick as far as he could in the direction of the camp, knowing his dog would chase after it. Well aware of his dog's short attention span, he was sure something else would distract it. And if the dog lingered near the camp long enough, maybe the boy would notice. Chico held his breath and waited to see what would happen.

The dog raced through the brush after the stick, but stopped when it spied an opossum rooting in the dirt. The dog sniffed the ground and crept closer to investigate, then started barking and jumping at the startled opossum. The opossum froze where it stood, and the dog kept barking.

Chico laughed. It couldn't have worked out better. His dog would bark at the motionless animal until something else caught the dog's eye. The racket would probably continue for some time. A barking dog would attract little attention from the adults who were dancing and celebrating, but he felt sure the one-eyed boy would notice. He knew he would if he were in the boy's place.

"Watch!" Chico told Jefe.

When the opossum finally came out of its startled trance, the dog began to thrash it about. The opossum, pulling away, lurched through the brush and then climbed the lone mesquite tree near the camp. Just as Chico had hoped, the boy glanced over, interested by the noise, and recognized the dog. He looked around. Then he snapped his fingers and whistled softly.

The dog bounded toward him and sniffed. It circled the boy, and then stopped to lick at something he held in his fingers. The boy scratched the dog's head and squinted through the smoky darkness. It didn't look as if he could see anything through the thick haze.

Chico whistled. The dog perked his ears and raced to answer. The boy watched it disappear in the dark. Then he raised his hand in their direction as a signal and turned back to tend the fires.

"I'll keep watch," Jefe announced. "Maybe they'll come tonight."

Chico doubted they would come so soon, and he was right. Many more nights passed. Each evening, Chico sent his dog toward the camp, and each evening the boy greeted him with a small bit of food. It seemed as if the dog took just a little longer each night to answer Chico's whistle, and that made Chico nervous. He hoped the sailors would make their escape before his dog decided to stay with the other boy.

Finally, one night the boy did not tend the fires. The dog wandered closer and closer to the camp, sniffing the ground, looking for his usual bit of food.

"Where's the boy?" Jefe asked anxiously. "Did he trick us? Are my men really still alive?"

Chico didn't answer. He had trusted the boy. He just hoped the dog's evening visits hadn't gotten the boy in trouble. They kept watching. Finally, just when Chico was about to whistle for his dog to return, they heard a low whistle from the other end of the thicket. The dog bounded off in the direction of the whistle.

Chico was suddenly terrified. Maybe this whole plan had been a trick after all. Maybe he shouldn't have trusted the boy. Maybe he had lost his dog. Maybe they were going to be trapped and forced to work as slaves with Jefe's men.

Chico's breath came short and fast with fear. His heart pounded. He gave a quick, panicked whistle for his dog.

There was a rustle of undergrowth and then quiet murmurs of low voices. Chico and Jefe moved far back in the shadows and waited, frozen.

The dog burst through the scrub brush. Barking and quivering with excitement, he headed straight for Chico. Behind the dog came the one-eyed boy and two men who were not Indians.

Jefe leaped from his hiding place and exclaimed, "Dorantes! Castillo! *Gracias a Dios!* Thank God!"

While the three Spaniards embraced, Chico stared at

the man who followed them. His skin was deep brown, nearly black. He was taller than the others and had a broad face and huge eyes. He flashed a smile at Chico, revealing large white teeth behind his wide lips. Chico had never seen such an amazing person. Instinctively, he relaxed and smiled back

"I must get back before my mother misses me," the Indian boy said. "I'll try to make excuses for these men if anyone is looking for them, but you should leave and get as far as you can tonight. Remember to go inland, not down the coast."

He tossed a last bit of food to the dog and cocked his head to look at Chico. "Thanks for sending him every night. He's a good dog. But don't let him follow me back," he warned. "Dogs don't always last long around our cooking fires."

Chico tried not to shudder at that awful possibility as he grasped the boy's arm in thanks. Then Estevanico reached out and wrapped his huge arms around the half-blind Indian boy.

"Thank you, little friend," his deep voice rumbled.

In the shadows cast by the full moon, the boy sneaked back to his camp while Chico and the others crept through the thicket and traveled inland. They made no fires because they didn't want the smoke to lead anyone to them. After two days and two nights, they decided the hostile Indians weren't coming after the fleeing captives.

"We did it! We got away!" Chico was relieved. Not only had they escaped the Indians, his dog had stayed close at his side and never even tried to go back to the other boy at the prickly pear grounds.

—

Their journey stretched first into days, and then into weeks. The three Spanish sailors walked together in different combinations, talking about their shipmates and what had happened to them. Chico always stood next to Jefe, eager to hear the bits of information that fell during those conversations. But today he walked behind the Spaniards, with Estevanico.

"We walk as if we know where we are going. Do we?" Estevanico asked.

Chico answered, "Jefe searches for the settlement of Spaniards down the coast at a place called Panuco. He's just trying to get back where he belongs."

"And you?" Estevanico. "What is your story?"

Chico looked surprised at his interest. Until now, they had usually walked in comfortable silence. "Me? I'm still looking for where I belong,"

"Where do you come from?" Estevanico asked.

"I come from an island village on the coast. After the shipwreck came the stomach sickness, and my family and many others died. There was nothing left for me there. I was treated badly by my aunt and uncle, so I left with Jefe. He's trying to find his old life, and I'm trying to find a new one." Chico shrugged and continued, "After you and Jefe return to your own people, I guess I'll have to keep looking on my own. We've been to many villages and met many people, and I don't seem to belong anywhere."

Estevanico looked puzzled. "But you belong wherever you are."

"What do you mean?" Chico was confused. "I don't really belong with Jefe. I'm just traveling with him because I have no one else. I have no other choice."

"Even a slave has choices," Estevanico replied, and then he paused. He had a peaceful manner about him and he spoke with a calm confidence. He thought a minute before he continued. "It's true; sometimes life takes us to unfamiliar places. But just because they're unfamiliar doesn't mean we don't belong there. We just have to find out *how* we belong there."

Chico still didn't understand. "But you're a slave. You belong to Dorantes. You don't have a choice where you go."

Estevanico shook his head. "As I said before, even a

slave has choices. He can choose his attitude and actions, no matter where he finds himself."

He paused and smiled down at the young man beside him. "And you? You have a whole new world right here. You don't need to find *where* you belong in this vast land; you only need to find out *how* you belong."

They walked again in silence. Chico wasn't sure what to think of this quiet man with the strange ideas. Estevanico picked up a stick and tossed it ahead for the dog to chase.

In and out of villages they wandered, and over great spaces where no one lived but animals. Chico could walk unnoticed among many of the people they met. But the Spaniards and Estevanico were different than anyone the villagers had ever seen. Around them, rumors grew up. From villagers, they began to hear things about themselves–that they came from the sun, or that they could not be killed. Chico could not help but smile at some of what he heard.

One morning, Jefe called out to Chico. "There is smoke up ahead." He pointed at the spires of smoke rising over the trees in the distance. "Take Estevanico and go see if it is a village where we might be welcome and allowed to trade for food. We'll wait here."

They were traveling in unfamiliar territory now and Jefe didn't want to take unnecessary chances with unfriendly villagers. They'd all been through too much to risk losing their freedom again.

Chico and Estevanico hurried ahead, but before he reached the group of huts, a man ran toward him, shouting in welcome. He waved his arms and gestured toward their fires. Then he said a curious thing. "We have heard that the men with you are children of the sun, and that they have the power to cure the sick." Estevanico raised his eyebrows. Chico tried to suppress a smirk.

The man continued. "We want you to prove it," he said.

Chapter 9

Chico stopped in his tracks. He wasn't sure he understood what the man was saying.

"We are traders," Chico began.

"You travel with the strangers who came from far away, don't you?" the man asked.

"Y-y-yes," Chico stammered, searching for the right words to explain who they were. "But they don't come from the sun or the sky. They're ordinary men–sailors who come from a country across the sea."

"We heard that they're children of the sun," the man insisted. "And we need them to heal some of our people. You are all welcome in our village, and we'll give you food to show our thanks."

Estevanico leaned close to Chico and spoke quietly. "This is not so crazy as it might sounds. Señor Castillo is the son of a doctor. He will know how to help these people," he said.

Chico thought about the villager's invitation. He was hungry and tired. For days he and the other four men had been making their way across rough, unfamiliar ground. It would feel good to stop and rest. It sounded as if they'd be safe in this village, but he wasn't at all comfortable about the Indians thinking the Spaniards had great healing powers.

Leaving Estevanico to wait with the villager, Chico ran back to take the message to the others. The three men agreed that they, too, were tired and hungry. Worse, they didn't know where they were or which direction they should travel to reach the Spanish outpost.

"If we're able to help their sick people, then maybe they will help us figure out the best route to Panuco," Jefe suggested.

Chico looked at Castillo. "Estevanico says that your

father is a physician. Is this true? Can you heal these people?"

Castillo nodded but seemed nervous. "I learned a few skills from my father, but I have no formal training. I'll look at their sick and see what I can do to help, but I make no promises."

The little group agreed to take a chance and accept the Indian's invitation. They joined Estevanico and the villager. "I think this man is the leader of the village," Estevanico explained. The man led them in the direction of the wisps of smoke ahead.

They reached the village at sunset. Chico didn't see any other dogs. He kept his own close by his side.

The little band of Indians had just returned from picking prickly pears in fields nearby. Some of the women were roasting the tunas. Others were squeezing the juice from the fruits into a hole dug in the ground. Chico watched them stir in a bit of dirt and then taste the mixture. It reminded him of his mother adding seasoning to a fish stew.

One of the women noticed the visitors and smiled. She gestured at Chico, inviting him to drink. He wasn't sure what it would taste like, but he was thirsty after the day's trek. A little nervous, he knelt beside the hole, and cupping his hand, he scooped up a handful of the purple juice. The sweet liquid tasted so good that he took a second handful and then a third.

When he'd finally quenched his thirst, he took a deep, satisfied breath. Seeing he'd enjoyed it, the woman reached over and patted his hand. Chico reacted with surprise. It had been a long time since he'd felt a mother's affectionate touch, and he'd forgotten how nice it was. He gave her a grateful smile.

Later, after the travelers had rested, the village leader brought several of the villagers to Castillo, asking him to cure their terrible headaches.

"They believe you can ease their pain," Chico translated for Castillo.

"We can only hope that if they truly believe it, maybe it will happen," Castillo answered. He hesitated. "Ask them to lie down and I will make the sign of the cross over each one."

"Our *shaman*, the village medicine man, always blew on a sick person's body. Maybe you should do that, too," Chico suggested.

"Thank you, Chico. I'll try everything. It certainly can't do any harm." Castillo knelt beside each of the patients. He made the sign of the cross and blew gently over each one. Then he raised his hands toward the sky and prayed, "Lord God, we commend these people to you and ask that you grant them good health. Amen."

Silence. Chico held his breath. Jefe and Dorantes stood tense and still. Only Estevanico appeared unworried as they watched and waited.

One by one, the Indians each rose, looked around, and smiled. They said they felt no more pain. Chico let out a sigh of relief. He didn't know what he had expected would happen if Castillo hadn't cured them, but he was glad he didn't have to find out.

Each of the healed Indians went home and returned with *tunas* and venison as gifts for the travelers. Chico hadn't eaten red meat in many months. He couldn't even remember the taste, but his mouth watered when he saw the deer meat. But before he got a chance to eat, more villagers came to ask for healing.

Chico, Estevanico and Castillo spent the evening working with any who asked for their help. Chico translated as well as he could, and Estevanico helped with some of the words he'd learned from his Indian captors. Each patient left declaring he had been healed and then returned with more gifts of food for the visitors. Afterwards, the whole village celebrated the cures with feasting and dancing until dawn.

Chico ate venison and drank the juice of *tunas* until his belly ached. The woman from the juice pit brought him a deer bone after she saw him toss a bit of meat to his dog. Chico thanked her with a big grin. The dog stayed at his feet the rest of the night, gnawing all the last bits of meat from the bone before cracking it open and licking at the marrow inside.

Later, the head man asked Chico to speak to Jefe for him. "We'll be going soon to gather the last of the prickly pear tunas and mesquite beans," he said. "It's a long walk from here. Please come with us. Our people would feel safer with you and your men along."

Jefe was enthusiastic about the plan. "We can explore the land if we go with them. We'll learn what food is available and where the rivers lead. I want to do anything that will help us find our way to a Spanish outpost," he said.

The ground was rough. The soil was hard and reddish beige. Beneath a sandy top layer was caliche, a hard mixture of sand and limestone. Dry gullies wound through the brush. It was hard, desolate country.

Once they reached the river, the people set up their lodges. The small, round huts reminded Chico of those used by the Karankawas. The head man pointed toward the thickets across the flat land before them. "Last year we found mesquite trees heavy with beans in that direction."

Chico was tired, but he was also hungry. He was ready to go find whatever food might be out there, so he immediately set out with Estevanico. They followed the head man and other villagers who walked in small groups of two or three. Castillo and Dorantes also followed, deep in conversation together, as usual. Jefe struck out on his own.

Little groves of mesquite dotted the brushy landscape. Chico and Estevanico stopped when they reached a group of several trees with spreading branches. Clusters of long brown bean pods hung among the feathery leaves. When the wind blew, the dry pods rattled against each other, reminding Chico of the rattlesnake's rattle. He shivered at the sound.

Chico reached for a handful of beans.

"Ouch!" he said. The tips of the pods were hard and sharp. The pods themselves were leathery and tough. They scratched his hands and arms. "This is as bad as digging roots," he moaned.

Estevanico watched Chico and grimaced. "This will be hard work, won't it?" he asked.

Chico nodded grimly. By the time the sun began to set, Chico's arms were bleeding where the thorny branches had scratched him. His hands were covered with cuts from the sharp beans. His neck and shoulders hurt from reaching to tug each clump of beans from the branches.

Worst of all, he was still hungry.

In the prickly pear fields, picking the tunas had been painful work, too. Stooping over to pull the small fruit from the spiny cactus had left him with an aching back and pricked fingers. But at least he'd never gone hungry while gathering the tunas. Anytime he wanted he could stop and eat as much of the juicy fruit as he pleased.

But, like the bitter roots he'd dug for his aunt, these dry mesquite beans weren't edible straight from the tree. They were too tough and bitter to chew without soaking them first. They'd make good flour when the women ground them up into fine bits. He'd even heard that they made a kind of tea by boiling the pods. But right now, he and Estevanico had a basket full of food they couldn't eat, and they were out in the middle of nowhere without any way to turn these mesquite beans into a meal.

"Let's get back to the camp," Chico suggested. "The sun is nearly down. Maybe some of the others have found something we can eat tonight."

Estevanico agreed, and the two headed back in the direction they'd come. They had walked in a straight line from the camp to the grove where they stopped to pick beans, so it wasn't hard to find their way back. When they arrived at the camp, Dorantes and Castillo were waiting.

"Where's De Vaca?" Castillo asked.

"Isn't he with you?" Estevanico questioned him.

"No, we thought he was with you, Estevanico," Dorantes answered. "Did you notice which direction he went?"

"No, I didn't even see him leave." He turned to Chico, "Did you see which way De Vaca went?" Estevanico asked.

"Who is De Vaca?" Chico answered. Then he gasped and put his hand over his mouth. "Is that Jefe's sacred name?" he asked in a nervous whisper.

The three Spaniards stared at Chico. Finally Estevanico asked him, "What are you talking about? What is a sacred name?"

"In Karankawa culture, each person has a secret name, given to him at birth, but never spoken. We use nicknames instead so that the bad spirits can't find out our real identities and steal our souls," Chico explained.

"Chico is not your real name?" Estevanico asked, surprised.

"No, it's just what Jefe calls me. He told me to call him Jefe. He never spoke about another name and neither did I," Chico answered.

The other men smiled. "That explains a lot," Castillo told Chico with Estevanico's help. "In our language, Chico means boy, and Jefe means chief. Jefe's given name is Alvar Nuñez Cabeza de Vaca. We don't believe in bad spirits.

It's all right to call him De Vaca. No harm will come to him."

"What should we call you?" Dorantes asked Chico.

Chico swallowed. He didn't want to be rude to these older men, but he did believe in bad spirits even if they didn't. He hesitated, and smiled nervously. "Please call me Chico."

The men nodded their understanding but then went back to their original question. Where was Jefe, as Chico preferred to call him? None of them had seen him since leaving camp. Estevanico and Chico asked the villagers, but nobody had noticed where he'd gone.

Chico looked across the drab landscape. The sun had almost completely slipped below the horizon and soon it would be very dark. There would be no moon this evening. Only a very small campfire would light the night.

"Surely," Chico said to Estevanico, "Jefe will find his way back to camp soon."

Estevanico said nothing, but his expression was solemn. Suddenly the boy was very frightened. He knew how dangerous it would be for Jefe to be out in the brush after dark.

Chico shuddered, remembering how the bean pods had sounded like a snake's rattle. It reminded him that there were real snakes out there. There were other wild animals as well, creatures that came out only at night. He'd heard stories about big cats with long claws that ripped apart their prey. Wild peccary–short-legged animals with long snouts and with sharp tusks–roamed at night. They were less fierce but they'd still attack if they felt threatened. Chico could hear wolves and coyotes howling in the distance. His dog whimpered at the sounds and leaned close against him.

Where was Jefe?

What would happen to him if Jefe never came back? Chico lay awake all night, waiting and wondering and worrying. Even surrounded by the sleeping villagers, he felt as afraid and abandoned as he had when his family died, leaving him on his own. He was reliving a nightmare. His uncle's words haunted him, "There is nothing left for you here."

What would he do if Jefe didn't ever return? Then there would be nothing left for him here, either. Chico knew that Castillo and Dorantes were good men, but they had no real interest in him or what happened to him. He was useful as an interpreter, but so was Estevanico. The slave belonged with them, but Chico knew he didn't.

He could probably stay at the village, but everything about it was so unfamiliar: the food, the language, the land itself. He'd still be alone and out of place. Once again he was facing the same problem that had followed him from his old home on the island: Where did he belong?

If Jefe didn't come back, Chico didn't know what he would do. Fear paralyzed him. He decided that all he could do was wait and hope for Jefe's return.

The group of Indians and Spaniards slept near the river that night and the nights that followed. They spent their days gathering the mesquite beans and the last prickly pear fruit of the season. And Chico waited and watched for Jefe.

Chico saw the villagers shake their heads. He heard them muttering about the foolish foreigner. "A snake probably bit him," one said. "More likely he's fallen into a gully and an animal got him," another suggested.

Chico longed to tell them it wasn't true, but day followed day, and still there was no sign of his friend.

After five days, the leader of the village approached Chico and Estevanico.

"Tomorrow we go back to the village. We've picked everything we can find here, and your man must be dead or he'd have returned by now," he told them. "The weather is changing. I can feel the wind shifting to the north. We need to get back to the safety of our village before the storm comes. You're welcome to spend the cold months with us and share what little we have, but there's no reason to stay camped by the river any longer. There's nothing left for us here."

"Nothing left...nothing left..." the phrase echoed in Chico's head, keeping rhythm with his pounding heart.

"What the head man tells us is true," Estevanico said to Chico. "There's nothing left for us here, and there's no reason to wait any longer for Jefe to come back."

He put his hand on the young man's shoulder and looked him in the eye. "I'm afraid he's gone, Chico."

Chico shook his head. He didn't want to hear Estevanico's words. He turned away and started running. He ran far down the riverbank into the brush, not caring what branches scratched him or what roots tripped him. He wanted to get as far away as he could.

The dog started out at Chico's side. But, thinking they were playing a game, it raced ahead and was soon out of sight. Chico could hear it yipping somewhere in the distance.

When his side began to hurt, Chico stopped to catch his breath and brush the sharp gritty dirt from his feet. He heard a voice calling to him, but he didn't want to talk to anyone right then. He didn't care who had followed him. He didn't want to hear what they had to say.

"Chico!" he heard again. The voice came from up ahead, not behind him. His heart raced. He strained to listen.

Chapter 10

"Chico!" he heard again. "Chico! It's me, Jefe! Where are you? Your dog has found me!"

Chico recognized the hoarse voice. He let out a whoop and pushed ahead through the brambles and brush, following the sound of his barking dog.

Jefe sat on a big, flat rock, the dog barking, yipping, and scampering around him. The older man looked tired and sunburned, but his eyes were bright. He smiled at Chico.

"Are you hurt? Are you all right?" Chico cried. "Where have you been? They told me you weren't coming back! I was afraid...I didn't know what..." He couldn't stop the torrent of words.

"I got lost. I wanted to explore a bit, but there are no trails out here and everything looks so much the same. It's all dry and brown and brushy," Jefe explained. "I guess I got mixed up trying to find my way back to the camp."

"But it's been five days!" Chico protested. "How did you survive? What did you eat?"

"It's been five very long days," Jefe agreed. "During all that time I did not eat a mouthful, and my bare feet bled a great deal. God had mercy upon me, otherwise I could not have survived."

"Yes, you're lucky that the weather held out, but that won't last much longer. Now it's turning colder. We need to get back to the village before the north wind blows in." Chico helped him to his feet.

"You say your God had mercy on you when you were lost," the boy said. "I'm glad." He paused before finishing. "It's frightening to be alone."

Jefe nodded, and Chico relaxed for the first time in five days.

Chico, Jefe, and the dog started to walk back toward the camp. Soon they met Estevanico. He had followed Chico when he ran away. The slave stopped and stared at the sight of Chico helping Jefe along the rough riverbank.

"Gracias a Dios!" Estevanico exclaimed. "Thank God you're alive! How did you ever survive, alone, in such a strange place?"

"I have to admit, once I realized I was really lost, I got scared," Jefe laughed sheepishly. "I imagined all kinds of dangers; this land is so strange and unfamiliar to me."

"So what did you do?" the slave asked as other villagers rushed up to join them.

Jefe took a deep breath, "Well, I knew I had to make a choice. I could listen to my fears, give up, and wait to die out there. Or I could keep walking and searching and take the chance I'd find my way back." Jefe shrugged. "I decided to keep going."

Chico hung his head. He didn't want the others to see the tears that burned his eyes. He was embarrassed and ashamed about how scared he'd been while Jefe was gone. Jefe had been in danger and afraid and alone, too, but the man had not given up. Instead, he had made the choice to keep looking, despite his fears, and he'd hung on to the slim chance of finding his way back. Chico, on the other hand, knew that he hadn't made the same choice himself. Full of fear about being left on his own, Chico had just given up. He had stopped and waited for someone else to do something instead of doing something himself.

"I was so afraid," he whispered to himself.

Jefe heard him and laid his hand on the boy's shoulder. "So was I, Chico, believe me," he assured him quietly. "But I've discovered that sometimes no matter how big your fears are, you're better off facing them and moving ahead. I'm glad I kept going. Otherwise I'd still be lost and waiting in the desert, instead of standing here with you where I belong."

Chico nodded. He wondered if he'd ever be as brave as Jefe.

"How did you stay warm?" one of the villagers called out. "The nights are cold without a fire."

"I'm glad you asked, because that's a very strange story," Jefe answered, giving Chico's shoulder a reassuring squeeze. "I stumbled across an old, dry bush that was on fire. Nobody was around. I can't explain it. Maybe it was an old campfire that had been left smoldering. Maybe the wind fanned the dying embers back to life. Wherever it came from, I was very glad to see it. After that, I carried a burning branch from it with me all the time so I would be able to light a fire wherever I stopped for the night. Then I covered myself with leaves and branches to keep warm while I slept." He paused and stroked his hair. "Look at this," he motioned.

The people leaned forward for a better look.

"You're burned!" Chico exclaimed.

Jefe laughed. "Only singed, but it could have been a lot worse. I didn't know about the night winds, so I never considered how dangerous it was to cover myself with dry leaves so close to a campfire. I was just trying to stay warm," he shook his head and the people chuckled. "I can see I still have a lot to learn about living in this new world."

Jefe recovered from his ordeal in the wilderness, and Chico and the Spaniards stayed in the village during the cold winter. Finally, when the weather warmed up again, the explorers left the village to continue their journey. As days widened into months, they trudged through rugged, desolate country and they hiked along mountains that rose up along the edges of great plains. Along their way, they passed through village after village. But they were not alone now. As they traveled through each new place, little knots of local people began to follow them. They didn't communicate much, but whenever Jefe, Chico, and the others looked back, villagers trailed after them in an ever-growing crowd. Each night was full of the sounds of quiet talk around many fires. Chico was baffled.

"Some of these people have been following us for

months!" he said one afternoon. "Why are they still there?"

"Disciples of the healer!" laughed Estevanico, nodding at Castillo. Castillo looked uncomfortable.

"I've seen them take tribute from other villagers as we pass through," said Dorantes. "Maybe they think we're not charging enough for Castillo's miracle healings. Maybe looking like a part of our little group is good business!" The men laughed. Castillo remained silent.

"Don't pay any attention to them, Castillo," said Jefe. "These people are following us because they're fearful about our safety."

"Safety?" said Chico.

"Can you blame them?" said Jefe. "Just look at us! Do we look like we could survive long out here?"

Chico had become accustomed to the ragtag appearance of their party. Now he looked again. What clothes they wore were tattered and worn. The Spaniards' beards were long and tangled, like Chico's own hair. He felt an odd sort of pity for his friends, and for himself.

"Besides," said Jefe, "I don't see them taking tribute from other tribes as much as I see them giving things of their own. There seems to be generosity on both sides."

On they went. They traded and cured in villages where the people ate different foods, built different kinds of houses, and kept different traditions than any of the tribes that lived nearer the seacoast. Chico had never known there could be so many different ways to live. Still, he kept looking for a place where he belonged.

At one village, two *shaman*, or medicine men, welcomed the travelers. Their tribe, like so many others, had heard stories about the travelers' healing powers and greeted them with gifts.

"As a token of welcome to our village, please take these gourds," the medicine men spoke as Chico translated. "They are symbols of your authority as healers." The shaman presented Chico with two large gourds. He passed them to Jefe and Estevanico. Each of the gourds was decorated with a string of bells and two feathers–one white and another red.

"Carry these with you," the shaman instructed, "and people will know you come in peace. They'll know you are men with the power to cure the sick." He lowered his eyes in respect and stepped back.

Chico bowed in return, and then repeated the instructions to Jefe.

Jefe said, "Please tell him we're honored by the gift." He nodded to the village medicine men. "And ask where they got these gourds. We haven't seen anything like them anywhere."

"They claim that these gourds have healing virtues, and that they come from Heaven," Chico explained to Jefe. "The rivers carry them down when they rise and overflow the land. They want us to know that it's a great honor to carry one. We should have no trouble with any tribe now, no matter where we go."

And that, Chico added to himself, was a great relief.

With their growing reputation as healers and traders, Chico and the Spaniards had traveled safely in recent months. Still, he and Jefe and the other three survivors were strangers in this country, and he'd never forgotten what the boy at the river had said about that. In some villages, it wasn't good to be different. Anyone different risked being treated badly.

But now that they carried the ceremonial gourds, their safety was guaranteed. The gourds assured them safe passage and respect throughout the land. Chico noticed that once they had the gourds, the villagers that had been following them began, over the course of many days, to wander away toward their own distant villages. Chico took even more comfort in this. After all, if the natives didn't feel fearful for their safety anymore, perhaps there was nothing to fear.

Still, as they traveled, there was never a lack of spectators. The people of each new village went out of their way to see the strangers as they passed through. And with the gourds came more demands for healing.

"Please cure my brother!" begged one man who offered beads, bison hides, and pine nuts. "He was shot with an arrow and the head of it is lodged in his chest. He hasn't been able to move without pain for a long time."

Chico relayed the message to the four Spaniards. Castillo's eyes widened.

"We can't cure a wound like that!" the sailor said. Chico heard the worry in his voice. "So far we've been lucky that all our patients have survived, but this sounds dangerous."

Dorantes agreed. "If we try to heal him and we fail, they'll blame us if he dies. We'll lose their trust and respect. I don't think we should even try. Who knows what they might do to us?"

Chico looked at Estevanico. The slave shrugged. "This is not for me to decide."

Jefe looked around at his men and laughed. "You have so much fear for men who have already survived so much! What's happened to your courage?" He turned to Chico and put an arm on his shoulder. "Take me to the man's brother. I've treated wounds like this in battle."

The man's brother lay motionless on a buffalo hide inside his smoky lodge. Chico watched as Jefe probed at the knot on the patient's chest. He watched the wounded man's face for a reaction, but the patient lay still and tense and didn't make a sound.

"This native shows more bravery than my own people," Jefe declared to Chico. "Tell him I'll have to cut the arrow head out from under his skin. Once it's out, he'll be able to move again without pain. But I won't lie. Getting it out is going to hurt a lot. Does he still want me to do it?"

Chico translated Jefe's question for the Indian, and the man nodded. Then he closed his eyes and seemed to slow his breathing as if he were in a trance.

Jefe beckoned to Chico. "I'll need your help with this."

Chico's skin crawled at the idea of cutting through a person's skin. He didn't see how Jefe could do it. He didn't want to help. He didn't want to be anywhere near the operation, but he also didn't want to let Jefe down. He gritted his teeth, took a deep breath and moved closer.

"Move around to his other side," Jefe directed. "After I cut through his skin, hold the wound open so I can reach in and pull out the arrow point."

Chico felt his stomach lurch as he watched Jefe slice open the man's skin. While Jefe set the knife aside, Chico pried the edges of the cut apart and held the skin open. Blood oozed and he had to press hard to keep his fingers from slipping. Jefe reached in and probed for the arrow's tip with his fingers.

"It's very deep," he announced. "I'll need to pry it out. Pass me the knife again."

Chico swallowed. He glanced at the patient who lay motionless with beads of sweat on his lip. Jefe used the knife to probe deeper and was able to loosen the arrowhead at last. Fingers slick with blood, he gently pulled the tip from the man's chest.

"It's much bigger than I thought it would be," he said to Chico. "No wonder he's been in so much pain."

The man's brother reached for the bloody arrowhead and held it up. "Can I take this?" he asked. "I want everyone to see what you've done."

"Of course," Jefe shrugged. He turned again to his patient. "We'll sew the skin back together now, and take out the stitches in a day or two. I'll stay with him until then to be sure he doesn't get a fever."

Jefe made two stitches with a deer bone needle, cleaned the sticky blood from the man's chest, and laid a deerskin over him. When it was all over, Chico wiped his hands on his legs to stop the trembling. He glanced at Jefe's hands, steady and sure. He marveled at the Spaniard's skill and daring. And he knew without a doubt the patient would survive.

The patient's brother took the arrowhead and showed

everyone. The whole village came back to look at it, and they sent it further inland that the people there might see it, too.

The people were amazed. They decided to hold a feast, and they began to plan a great *mitote*, or celebration. Rihóy, the chief hunter, announced they would make a special hunting trip to bring back meat, maybe deer or bison, for the festivities. They would leave at dawn and return in two days.

"You should go with them," Jefe told Chico. "It's time you learned to hunt big game."

Secretly, Chico longed to do just that. Still, he felt responsible for helping Jefe with his patient. "Don't you need my help?" he asked.

Jefe waved away his concern. "Estevanico can help me." He added, smiling, "Besides, you can help best by learning how people hunt in this region. If we're going to survive in this new land, we'll need the wisdom and skills of the natives when we're hungry on our travels."

Chico was excited. He jumped up and whistled for his dog, who was out somewhere wandering idly around the village. Chico stopped to wonder if the dog might be a hindrance on the hunt, but then he decided to take him anyway. Maybe the dog would learn something, too.

The hunters and several women gathered at the edge of

the village before dawn the next morning. Chico was glad to see another boy his age, as well as a few dogs besides his own. The men each carried a bow and arrows, and some carried clubs. Others carried torches.

They struck a trail to the north. Chico's dog joined the little pack of dogs running along together, enjoying the chance to romp in the morning air. The men seemed just as excited about the outing as the dogs. They walked together in groups of two or three, talking and laughing.

Chico walked alone until another boy joined him. The other boy was shorter than he, and a little younger, but he was sturdy and strong. Chico smiled at him. He reminded him of his old friend, Mano.

"They call me Chico," he said after they'd walked along in silence for a few minutes.

"I am called Micá," the other boy replied. "Is that your dog?" he asked, pointing toward the animals rambling through the grass.

Chico nodded. "He's a good dog. He's traveled with me all the way from the sea coast," he answered.

"You've seen the sea?" the boy asked with an envious tone. "You're so lucky!"

The boy at the river of nuts had used those same words. Chico still didn't see anything lucky about his life. He shrugged. "Well, I don't know about that. But I'm sure lucky to get to go on this hunt. I've never hunted anything bigger than rabbits and birds."

"I've never been on a hunt before, either," Micá admitted. "Maybe we'll find some bison. That would be more exciting than deer, wouldn't it?"

Just before nightfall, Rihóy, the leader, spotted a group of bison grazing in the distance. He gathered the hunters around him to give directions.

"Tonight we'll make our camp here," Rihóy announced. "That way the bison will grow accustomed to our scent blowing downwind. Then our movements won't alarm them. In the morning, just before the sun rises, we'll light a grass fire around them to drive them toward that narrow draw," he pointed, "between those rocky ridges to the west. We'll have hunters waiting to shoot them before the animals can find their way out."

Chico and Micá talked far into the night. For a long time they were both too excited to sleep. Chico's dog, however, was exhausted from the day's long walk. He lay dozing against Chico's leg. Finally, there was a lull in the conversation. Micá reached over to scratch the dog's head.

"Chico?" he said.

"Hmmm?" Chico answered absently. He was lost in thought. He had just told Micá about his father and his uncle and how they had hunted for fish in the bay with their bows and arrows. Now he was wondering what they would think about these huge bison grazing down the slope. He remembered how excited Mano had been about finding turtle eggs. He'd be amazed by this bison hunt.

"Are you scared?"

"I hadn't thought about it, but I don't think so," Chico replied truthfully. "Don't worry," he advised his new friend. "It's going to be exciting." And then, with a smile and his memories, he rolled over and slept at last.

—

"There are a few bulls, and many more cows," the leader announced early the next morning. "Aim for the cows first. We could make good use of the big, thick bull hides, but the cows' meat will be more tender than his."

Chico watched several men walk down the slope and disappear into the gray dimness of dawn. All he could see was their burning torches bobbing toward the grazing bison herd. They made almost a complete circle around the animals, and then dropped their torches to the ground, lighting the undergrowth and surrounding the bison with a ring of fire.

The bison reacted quickly to the scent of smoke. The bulls bellowed and led the cows away from the approaching flames. As the fire grew and closed in behind them, the bison picked up their pace. In minutes, they were thundering toward the only narrow open space in front of them. The hunters crept as close as they could and waited.

Chico watched, breathless. He held his bow firmly. He placed his arrow tight against the bowstring and sighted down the arrow's cane shaft. The sun had risen above the horizon now, and he could clearly see the action unfolding in the dawn's growing light. The men who had lit the fire now ran alongside the bison, waving sticks and shouting. The dogs joined them, barking and chasing the huge animals toward the narrow draw where they'd make easy targets.

Closer and closer the bison came. Their hooves pounded the earth like waves pound the shore. Chico felt the pulsing rhythm as they drew closer. Soon he could hear their snorting and heavy breathing as they raced in panic from the flames. Their eyes were wild with fear. They barreled past the first hunters and through a barrage of arrows.

Chico was ready. He chose one animal and kept his eye focused on its huge, furry head. When it came into range, Chico pulled back his bowstring and let the arrow fly. In the flurry of arrows, he couldn't see if he had hit his target or not. But there was no time to wonder. More bison thundered through the gauntlet of hunters. Chico put another arrow to his bow and shot at another animal. He shot again and again.

By the time the small herd passed, Chico had used all his arrows. Four bison in all, three cows and a bull, lay dying along their path. The others had broken through the deep brush and escaped through the thicket that blocked the draw.

Safe from the stampede, the men approached the bison. Chico and Micá were still shaking with excitement. They grinned at each other. "Let's go see!" Micá waved his arm to hurry Chico.

Chico ran along with him, but he couldn't see through the huddle of hunters already gathered around the animals. When he got closer, Chico heard a rumble of discussion, shouted questions, arguing voices. Finally, he saw Rihóy climb atop a big boulder, holding a fistful of broken arrows out for all to see. From their markings and feathers, Chico recognized them as his own.

"Who shot these arrows?" the leader demanded.

Chapter 11

Chico froze. He didn't know what was going on. In some villages, broken arrows were a sign of anger or war. Why had Rihóy broken his arrows?

Micá whooped in excitement. "Those are yours, aren't they, Chico?"

The hunters turned around to stare. Micá jumped up and down and pointed at his friend. "They're his! They're Chico's arrows!" He grabbed Chico's arm and tried to pull him forward.

Chico didn't know what to say. Should he answer truthfully, or just keep quiet? He didn't know what to do.

Then he heard one of the men say, "That's the boy who translates for the medicine men, isn't it?"

"He's no boy if these are his," the leader declared solemnly. He climbed down from the boulder and approached Chico. "Did you truly shoot these arrows?"

Chico swallowed nervously and nodded. What did a handful of broken arrows mean to these people? Had he done something wrong? Had he caused some kind of trouble without meaning to?

Jefe and the others were not there to help him. Even his dog was across the clearing, sniffing at the bison carcasses that the women were already beginning to skin and butcher.

Chico took a deep breath. He was on his own.

"Yes," he announced firmly. "I shot those arrows." He heard several men murmur to each other. "I'm sorry if I did something wrong," he explained. "I don't yet know the ways of your people and would never offend you on purpose." He looked down to show his respect.

"You have not offended us," Rihóy assured Chico. Then he asked, "Where is your father?"

Again, Chico was confused. He didn't understand.

"My father was called Behma, but he is dead, along with my whole family. I was left alone, so now I travel with the Spanish sailors, helping them with trading and healing."

"Then I would be proud to call you my son," the leader said. "We pulled one of your arrows from each of the dead bison. They were shot with such power that they were too deep to pull out without breaking. You must be a very good hunter, yet you wear no tattoos to tell of your great skills."

"I've never hunted anything except rabbits and birds before," Chico admitted. "I was still a boy when my father died."

"You have proven yourself a man today," Rihóy announced. "I would be honored to draw the markings on you myself at the *mitote*, the great feast. Our village has much to celebrate since you and your friends have joined us!"

—

Chico, Micá, and the hunters returned to the village in a loud, boisterous group. The dogs raced ahead, playing and chasing each other through the dry grasses. The women came last, loaded down with the butchered carcasses carefully wrapped up in the buffalo hides.

Chico immediately looked for Jefe. He found the

Spaniard where he expected, tending his patient. The Indian sat by the fire, talking to his brother while Jefe watched. He looked up and smiled when Chico entered.

"How was the hunt? Did you see any bison? Did you bring back fresh meat?" Jefe asked.

"How is the man doing? Did his wound heal? Have you removed the stitches?" Chico asked at the same time.

The two laughed at each other's eager questions. They sat and talked for a long time. Jefe told about his relief that the patient had recovered without fever. Even better, he said, the man could move without pain for the first time in many months.

Chico told Jefe about his part in the bison hunt. "The chief hunter says I should carry the markings of a hunter because I shot so well on the hunt," Chico began proudly. Then he hesitated. "And he wants to honor me as his own son at the *mitote*. I don't know what to do. Is this right? Does it show disrespect to my own father if I let him honor me in this way at the celebration?"

Jefe smiled again. "Any man would be proud to call you his son, Chico," he said. "You show no disrespect to your father. In fact, the chief hunter's offer honors not only you, but also your father's spirit that lives on in you."

Chico hadn't thought of it that way. He thought he'd been abandoned and alone all this time. He'd never realized that he carried his father's spirit with him. It was a new thought, and it felt good to him.

The dog yipped at the door of the lodging. Chico looked out. The sun had set while he and Jefe talked, and now he smelled fires and roasting meat. He heard mothers sending their children on errands to prepare for the feast.

"I'll be there shortly," Jefe said. "You should go now."

Chico and his dog found Micá close to the main bonfire at the center of the village. "You'll be tattooed tonight," Micá said. "Are you scared?"

Chico laughed. "I don't think so. Should I be scared?"

"I hear it hurts," Micá answered. Then he told him again, "You're so lucky!"

Chico just grinned. "Yes," he agreed this time. "I think maybe I am."

The celebration lasted all night. The feasting continued until a special drink was prepared and passed among the hunters. It was brewed from a plant that was unfamiliar to Chico, and after he drank the tea he felt giddy and happy. The women stayed in the shadows, cooking more food and drink.

At one point, late in the evening, Rihóy pulled Chico to stand by the center fire. The village shaman brought herbs and rubbed Chico's face, arms, and chest with the leaves. Something in the herbs made his skin tingle so he didn't feel the sharp shell knife when the chief hunter made quick incisions on his cheeks, his chin, his arms, and his chest. Then the men rubbed charcoal deep into the cuts, leaving designs that would remain for the rest of his life.

"These markings show your skill as a hunter," Rihóy declared when they finished, pointing to Chico's arms. "These show you are a man," he pointed to Chico's face. "And these show that I look on you as my own son," he pointed to Chico's chest.

"You honor me," Chico replied. The fresh tattoos were beginning to sting, and he tried to keep his voice from shaking. "You honor my father, Behma, as well. We thank you." He looked down to show respect to the older man. He hoped he had chosen the right words.

The chief hunter grasped Chico's arm and announced, "We are proud to include you in our village."

The meaning of older man's statement stunned Chico. And then a warmth began to spread throughout his body as Rihóy's words sank in. After so much searching, Chico had finally found the place where he belonged.

"Thank you," Chico answered with feeling. Then he straightened his shoulders. He stood tall. He felt strong. He knew without any doubt he was making the right choice when he replied, "I am proud to join you."

A shout of approval rose from the crowd. Drumbeats

and dancing began. Rihóy led Chico to a place in the circle of hunters swaying in time to the rattles and drums. Chico saw Jefe nod at him and leave the fire.

The *mitote* continued as the villagers celebrated. Chico danced with the other men around the fire deep into the night. He glimpsed Micá watching from the edge of the firelight. Micá grinned and gave a whoop as he punched the air with his fist. With a start, Chico remembered when he and Mano had shown their excitement with the same gesture at another feast so long ago.

A lifetime ago.

Chico instinctively kept the rhythm of the dance while his mind wandered back to his life as a boy on the island. He was amazed at what a different person he was now. A great deal of time and space separated Chico, the boy, from the man he'd become.

Chico blinked to bring his mind back to the present. Another hunter stepped beside him to offer his congratulations, "We are lucky to have you join us, Chico," the man said. "We need strong young hunters like you. Too many of our best hunters are getting old and can't keep up the way they used to. It's good to have young leaders like you step in to meet the needs of our people."

After nodding respectfully, Chico considered the man's words. A leader. The others saw him as a leader. How could this be possible? How had he gone from a frightened boy, lost and alone, to a leader, rich with new family and friends who needed him?

Jefe.

Of course! Chico thought to himself. The man had led him, step by step, from childhood to manhood. He'd shown him how to be a man. He'd helped Chico find his way to a place where he belonged, a place where he could stand on his own, secure and no longer afraid. It was a place where he could help others find their way now, just as Jefe had helped him.

"Please excuse me," Chico said abruptly as he bowed and left the circle of dancers. He wanted to thank Jefe, and he hurried from the fire to find him.

Jefe lay dozing by the fire outside his patient's hut. Chico's dog scampered ahead, and sniffed at the older man. It licked his face. Jefe opened his eyes, smiled, and reached to scratch the dog's head. "Hey," he laughed.

Chico reached the fire and squatted beside them. He hesitated; he didn't know how to begin. And then Jefe spoke first.

"The man is healing well," he said, gesturing toward the hut. "He'll be fine. We can leave tomorrow."

Chico's eyes widened. He hadn't thought Jefe would leave so soon. To be honest, Chico realized, in the excitement of the last hours he hadn't really thought about Jefe leaving at all.

"Leaving?" Chico asked. "Tomorrow?"

"Yes, I think we should go while the weather is good." Jefe stopped scratching the dog's head and looked at Chico. "Why? Isn't that what you came to ask?"

"No," Chico said. He took a deep breath and settled on the ground next to Jefe. "I came to talk about something else, but now I don't know where to start." He picked up a stick and threw it to the dog.

"Chico, what is it?" Jefe studied the troubled expression on the young man's face. Chico felt Jefe staring at him, and reached up to touch his new tattoos.

Jefe smiled. "They make you look different somehow," he remarked. "Older, maybe."

Chico hesitated again, and then decided to speak. He tried to choose his words carefully. "I *am* different," he began. "And I came to thank you."

"Thank me?" Jefe was puzzled. "For what?"

"For helping me find my way," Chico said. "For teaching me how to be a man. You've shown me how to face my fears, how to learn from my experiences, and how to respond when others need help. You've taught me what it means to make hard choices." Chico paused and looked Jefe in the eye. "This is one of those hard choices."

"What do you mean?" Jefe was still.

"I won't be going with you tomorrow," Chico said. "I've finally found what I was looking for, and I have you to thank for that."

"After one successful buffalo hunt you're ready to end your journey?" Jefe asked.

"It's more than that, Jefe," Chico answered patiently. "This is where I belong. It's what I've been searching for. I don't need to travel any farther. I have a new life ahead of me right here."

"I don't understand," Jefe shook his head. "How can you be so sure it's what you really want?"

"I felt something on that hunt," Chico said. His eyes were bright. "It felt right to be part of the group. I had a place. My presence mattered. My contribution made a difference. I actually helped the village. Me. On my own." Chico stood up and walked to the fire. He turned around to face Jefe again. "They need me. I have skills that can help this village grow and thrive."

"I'm valued. I'm needed," he repeated. "And," he added. "I'm happy here. I've decided to stay."

In the silence that followed, Chico paced in front of the fire before returning to sit beside Jefe again. The dog came up and nudged its way between the two men. They sat quietly while the animal thumped its tail back and forth against them. Jefe picked up a twig and broke it into pieces while he stared into the fire. Finally he spoke.

"It's your decision, Chico," he began. "And I do understand why you've made it. It's plain what a fine young man you've become, and the people here are lucky to have you join their family. It truly is a good place for you. You'll make a big difference in the life of this village. You have skills and wisdom they need," Jefe said. "The problem is I've come to depend on your skills and wisdom, too."

Chico blinked. He didn't know what to say.

"When we left the island, I was sure I knew everything about leading an expedition across this new world," Jefe went on. "After all, I'm an explorer. I'm a sailor. I'm a soldier. I have years of experience in new and strange places. But this land turned out to be different. There are obstacles here I've never encountered. The food, the people, the traditions–the land itself is completely unfamiliar to me, and I could never have survived this journey without the native knowledge and help you gave me."

"But–" Chico protested.

Jefe held up his hand to stop him. "Let me finish," he said quietly. "I may have taught you many things about being a man, but you taught me the value of the people who live in this new world. I'm a better man because of you."

"I'm proud to know that Rihóy has welcomed and accepted you as family," Jefe admitted. "Now you've found what you've been looking for, but I still need to find my way back to my own countrymen. I'll leave in the morning, with or without you, but you should know that these villagers are not the only people who have come to depend on you."

The two men sat silent again. Then Chico reached out his hand and clasped Jefe's arm. "I will see you off in the morning," he said simply before leaving the fireside.

—

Jefe checked on his patient one last time and then hurried to the edge of the village where Estevanico and the two other sailors already waited.

"Where's the boy?" Castillo asked. "We need to get on our way."

"He's staying here," Jefe said. "Let's go. There's no reason to wait."

Estevanico raised his eyebrows in surprise. "Are you sure?"

"I spoke with him last night. He's made his decision," Jefe said. "Let's go." He squinted at the rising sun and started walking. He was still in sight of the small village when he felt a familiar wet nose against his leg. Then

Chico's dog gave a yip and bounded ahead.

Jefe looked back. Hurrying to catch up were Chico and Rihóy. Jefe waited for them to approach. Then he stepped forward to speak to Rihóy.

"Thank you for your hospitality," Jefe said. "We tried to leave quietly. I'm sure everyone is still sleeping after last night's celebration and feasting."

Rihóy nodded in response to Jefe, "We were honored by your visit." Then he turned to Chico. "Be safe, my son," he said.

Jefe was confused. He looked at both men.

Chico spoke first and explained. "I talked with Rihóy after I left you last night," he said. "He agreed with my decision."

"To stay?" Jefe asked.

"No, I decided to go with you after all," Chico answered. "It was a hard choice to make. This is my home now. But now that I've found it, I understand how important it is to you to find your way home, too. As a man, I have a responsibility to help you, just like you helped me. Besides," he added with a grin, "you and I–and my dog–started this journey together, and I think we should finish it together."

Rihóy placed his hand proudly on Chico's shoulder and said to Jefe, "As a father, I ache to see Chico leave, but as a leader, I understand that he also has a responsibility to others outside his family. I know you can depend on him. We hope he will return home to us after helping you find your way back to yours."

The chief then said to Chico. "Learn all you can about the land beyond our village. Come back with stories and treasures from the rest of your journey. I want to hunt with you again soon."

"And so do I!" called Micá, panting as he ran to catch Chico before he left. "Maybe next time some of my arrows will actually hit something," he laughed. "And take care of your dog!" he called as he watched them disappear down the trail.

Chapter 12

The men and the dog traveled for many days. They crossed rivers and came to villages where the houses had flat roofs and thick walls made of mud.

"These people stay in one place and build sturdy homes," Chico told Jefe, translating for the villagers who greeted them. "The soil is rich and they plant crops in the nearby fields."

Jefe nodded. "I see they have plenty of corn and squash.

They probably only go out on short hunting trips when they need meat."

"They noticed the medicine gourds you carry and have invited us to stay with them tonight," Chico told Jefe.

Jefe spoke with the other Spaniards before turning back to Chico. "Tell them we'll be glad to stay. Castillo has noticed the clouds building up. It will be better for us to stop here rather than keep going and be caught in a storm."

Castillo was right about the weather. A storm blew in that night and it rained for fifteen days.

The river rose higher and higher along its banks. No matter how anxious Jefe was to continue their journey, it was impossible to cross the raging river and it was too dangerous to leave the village by any other route. The gullies and creek beds which criss-crossed the whole area were all swollen with angry floodwaters. The travelers spent the long rainy days inside the sturdy houses, healing the sick villagers, trading food and other goods, and telling stories to pass the hours.

During this time Castillo saw, on the neck of an Indian, a little buckle from a sword belt, and in it was sewed a horseshoe nail.

"Where did you get the buckle that's on your necklace?" Castillo asked him, pointing.

The Indian seemed strangely nervous about the Spanish

sailor's attention. He moved closer to Chico instead.

"Ask him who gave it to him," Castillo insisted.

"Some men came to the river," the man began. He looked at Chico, who nodded his encouragement. "They had beards like theirs," he gestured at Castillo, Dorantes, and Jefe.

The Spaniards looked at each other. Jefe raised one eyebrow as if he were surprised and curious to hear more.

"They came charging up on horses, huge snorting beasts. The men waved lances and swords at us, threatening us and demanding food," the man continued. "We told them we didn't have any with us, and that made them so angry that they killed two of our men without any warning. They laughed and trampled the men's bodies, and then they raced away in the direction of the sea." He swallowed and looked down. "I found this buckle on the ground after they were gone. It must have fallen from one of the horsemen. I wear it for protection in case they ever come back."

The man's story horrified Chico. He looked at Jefe. The older man seemed intrigued, but he wore a worried expression.

"This could be good news. It sounds like the man was describing Spanish soldiers, so now I'm more certain we're traveling the right direction," Jefe began. He frowned and muttered to himself, "But I don't understand why any Spanish soldiers would just ride in and treat the native people like that. What arrogance to think they have any right to threaten and harm innocent people! Why would soldiers think they have the right to come to this land and take over?"

His voice trailed off as he stared into the distance. Suddenly he closed his eyes and his face went pale. He shuddered as if he were cold. Then Jefe put his hand to his forehead and staggered to sit on a boulder nearby

"Can this story be true?" Chico asked. "Are you sure these are the men you're looking for? Do you know these men he told about?"

"If they were truly Spanish soldiers–and this man's necklace with the buckle proves they were–then I am ashamed to say that I know men like them," Jefe admitted, his head in his hands. "I'm even more ashamed to tell you that I was just like them not so long ago."

"What? You were never cruel to anyone in any village we visited," Chico argued.

"No, but only by the grace of God," Jefe answered. "If we hadn't shipwrecked on your island and lost everything," he began and shook his head. Then he started again, "If we had landed on your coast in our magnificent ships as we had planned, I would have come ashore with horses and armed men and no understanding of the native people, exactly like the soldiers this Indian just described. We were sent to take possession of this land for the King, and we thought that meant our mission was to conquer and destroy the people who already lived here. How could I have been so blind?"

Chico's eyes were huge.

"*Gracias a Dios, gracias,*" Jefe raised his head and Chico saw the tears on his cheeks. "Thank God we didn't get the chance. If not for that shipwreck leaving me helpless and dependent on the natives for my very life, I would never have seen just how wrong we were."

"Is everyone in your country like this?" Chico asked. He couldn't imagine such people.

"No, all Spanish are not like that, Chico," Jefe assured him. "Just as all Indians are not like the cruel ones who treated us badly or who made slaves of Castillo and Dorantes. I'm afraid no matter what tribe or country they come from, some men don't see that fear and cruelty are tools of hatred and conquest, not tools of peace and cooperation."

Chico thought about what Jefe said. There were cruel men and good men of every kind. He could accept that, but he wasn't sure where that left them right now.

"What do we do now?" he asked. "Do we keep looking

for them?"

"We keep going. We'll find the Spanish outpost soon, I'm sure, and we'll make them understand they are not to kill Indians, or make them slaves, or do any other harm," Jefe said. "My orders should be enough to stop any cruelty to the natives. It's been a long time, but I believe I still speak for the King. I know he wants this new world to prosper and grow. He needs loyal subjects to make that happen, not frightened, beaten-down slaves."

When the rain finally stopped and the river went down, Chico and Jefe and the others left the village. Along the way they began to see signs that other Spanish soldiers had been there before them. Tracks from horses were left along the trail. There were remains of recent campfires.

Chico was amazed at the landscape now. The grasses and trees were greener than any they'd seen on their long journey. There were lots of streams, and the dog splashed its way across every one.

The trail was easy, the land was rich, but the villages were empty. Some of the lodges were even burned to the ground. They saw no people until they finally came across one old man, digging through a partly burned stack of animal hides. He looked startled when he saw them come near.

"Where are your people?" Chico asked him. "What

happened here?"

"They've all fled to the mountains to hide from the Spanish soldiers," he told Chico. He saw the medicine gourds hanging on Jefe and Estevanico's walking sticks. "Are you the healers that I've heard about?"

"Yes, and we're looking for shelter and food," Chico answered. He didn't want to add that they were also looking for the Spanish soldiers.

"I'll take you where the other villagers are hiding in the woods, but we don't have much food to share," he warned Chico. "We haven't been able to grow anything since the Spanish came. We're afraid to plant any corn in our fields or gather any food. They burned our village and took half the men and all the women and children. Anyone who managed to get away is still hiding. I only risked coming back to see if there was anything left we could use. We left with nothing."

As he talked, the old man led Chico's group up a steep trail almost to the top of a mountain. The people hiding there were happy to see the healers. They brought out what little food they had, and everyone shared, but they had no fires. They were afraid the light and smoke would attract the attention of the Spanish soldiers. The villagers acted terribly frightened and begged Jefe to help them, telling their tales of cruelty at the hands of the Spanish.

Finally, Jefe spoke to Chico, "I've heard enough. It makes me sick to know my own countrymen would treat these people so badly." He sounded tired and sad. "I need you to do something for me, Chico," he said.

Chico nodded and waited. He didn't know what to expect.

"I need to stay here and help these people. All they want is to return to the peaceful life they had before the soldiers began raiding their villages. Because we carry the gourds, they think we can protect them with magical powers, and they're begging me to stay until it's safe for them to go back to their village," Jefe began. "Estevanico can translate and speak for me, but I want you to go back down the trail and be my eyes."

"What do you mean?" Chico asked.

"Stay in the woods and look along the trail for signs of the soldiers. Go as far as you can, spend the night and watch for their fires. Then come back and tell me if you have seen either Indians or soldiers anywhere."

At first, Chico felt nervous about going out alone. Absently, he reached down to scratch his dog's head, and in that motion he glimpsed the tattoos on his arm, signifying his strength as a hunter. He smiled at the reminder. It gave him confidence.

"I'll be back tomorrow with news," he told Jefe. He

grasped the older man's arm and clapped a hand on his shoulder.

"I know I can count on you," Jefe said. "Be careful."

Chico and his dog set out immediately. He kept the dog close at his side. He figured both of them were safer that way.

Once he reached the bottom of the steep trail, he crept through the trees. He soon discovered many signs that the soldiers had traveled that direction. He even saw stakes where he assumed horses had been tied. He'd never seen any horses himself, but Jefe had described the tall beasts that the soldiers rode in Spain. He could see where they had grazed and saw their droppings drying on the ground.

Late in the night, dozing under a large tree, Chico woke with a start. He heard an owl hoot above him and then the soft rustle of the branches as the night bird rose and flew into the night.

His eyes were drifting closed again when he heard something in the distance. It was a steady clatter, something like the rhythmic instruments used in the dances at a *mitote*. Then he heard sharp calls, then low moans. At first he thought the sounds were the chatter of squirrels, the sharp cry of a jay, and the soft call of the mourning dove.

But it was the middle of the night.

He listened more closely and strained to peer through the branches that separated him from the trail. He held a firm hand on his dog's neck; he could feel a low growl building there.

Figures came into view. Chico's eyes widened. His heart pounded. His mouth went dry. Soldiers on horseback led a group of Indians, chained together, crying in the night.

Suddenly, the dog struggled from Chico's grasp and ran, growling, toward the startled horses. The surprised animals wheeled about, whinnying and snorting in surprised confusion.

As Chico watched, the dog got tangled between one of the horse's back legs. He heard a yip as the horse tripped and kicked with its sharp hooves. By the time the horse regained its footing, Chico realized the dog lay limp at the side of the trail.

"No-o-o-o!" Without thinking of his own safety, Chico ran from the woods. Focused on his injured dog, he never saw the long lance swinging toward him. But he felt the hard crack on his forehead. He fell back. A roar filled his ears.

And then everything went black.

When he came to, Chico sat slumped on the back of a horse. He discovered that he was tied to a Spanish soldier sitting in the saddle in front of him. It was dawn, and they rode across a grassy plain. His head pounded and the dim sunlight hurt his eyes. With some effort, Chico managed to twist around enough to look over his shoulder. He saw the blurry outline of the woods fading behind them.

The soldier felt him move and turned around. "You're finally awake," he sneered.

"Yes," Chico replied. "What happened to my dog?"

The soldier was astonished. "You speak Spanish?" he asked in surprise.

"Some," Chico answered. "Where's my dog?" he demanded again through clenched teeth.

"Probably lying back in the woods somewhere, the clumsy thing," the soldier said with a wave of his gloved hand.

Chico felt his stomach rise in his throat. He said nothing.

Keeping his face expressionless, Chico watched dirty, exhausted Indians trudge past. He recognized them from the night before.

"Hey, Diego," the soldier called.

Another man on horseback rode up. "So, the savage is awake?" he laughed.

"Yes, I'm awake," Chico spoke up, hoping he sounded stronger than he felt.

"He speaks our language? How can this be, Mateo?"

Diego asked the other man.

"I've traveled with sailors from Spain for many, many months, searching for the outpost at Panuco. Their names are Castillo, Dorantes, Estevanico, and Jefe. I mean," Chico paused, searching his memory for the Spanish name, "Cabeza de Vaca."

The soldiers looked at Chico, stunned. Then they laughed. "That's impossible," Diego said. "Those men were lost at sea years ago."

"Yes, that's true," Chico insisted. "They were lost and then they shipwrecked on the island where I lived. It's a long story, but we've been traveling together since then."

"Those men are noblemen," Mateo, the first soldier, snorted. "They would never travel with a savage like you."

"Then how is it I can speak their language?" Chico reminded them.

"I have no idea, but I know you're a liar. You were alone when we caught you," Diego said. "Maybe you were their slave, and you escaped. Or maybe you killed them. Is that what happened?"

Chico bristled but stayed calm. "They're looking for you," he said. "I was sent ahead to see if we were on the right path. They'll follow soon, and then you'll know the truth."

One of the chained Indians cried out as he shuffled

beside the horsemen. "These men are cruel," he shouted to Chico. "They're taking us to sell as slaves!"

"Help us!" cried another.

"What did they say?" snapped Diego.

What could he do? How could he help them? He didn't belong in this horrible situation, bound and held as a slave, but he remembered Estevanico telling him that even a slave can make choices. He was sure that Jefe would look for him when he didn't come back to the mountain hideout. In the meantime, Chico's only tool was his knowledge of languages. Chico looked back at the desperate Indians and made his choice. He chose to speak for them; he would help these captives however he could.

"He said they're thirsty, hungry, and tired," Chico told Diego without hesitating. "When can they stop?"

The soldiers believed his translation. They hadn't let the natives stop for food or water for hours. "Tell them we'll stop when the horses need the rest. The animals are a lot more valuable than the captives," Mateo laughed. "There aren't any other horses around here, but Indians are easy to replace."

Easy to replace? Chico thought angrily. What kind of evil men were these Spanish soldiers?

"Stay strong!" he called to the Indians in their own language. "Help is on the way!"

With that, the soldiers were satisfied that he had given their message, and the Indians were hopeful that someone was coming to help them. Mateo untied Chico and shoved him to the ground so Diego could attach him to the front of the group of captives.

"We want you nearby so you can give them our orders," Diego told him. "It was lucky for us when you ran out after your dog. We might just have to keep you ourselves to help us raid the villages instead of shipping you to Spain with the others to be sold."

Chico didn't say anything. His vision had cleared, but his head still throbbed. He lifted it proudly anyway and glared at the soldier. Diego slapped him. "Don't get any ideas!" the soldier said before mounting his horse. "And keep up!"

They marched for hours. Step by weary step they stumbled along the trail. They paused once at a stream to water and rest the horses. While the horses grazed on the bank, the captives tore leaves and twigs from bushes and ate them eagerly. Some even peeled back the bark from trees and picked worms and beetles from underneath.

"When is help coming?" one asked Chico when the soldiers weren't paying attention. "What village will send people to save us?"

"Have you heard of the healers, the strangers who travel

between villages, trading and curing the sick?" Chico asked. Several knew of them.

"They are my friends. I was traveling with them," he said. "They'll come and save us. They'll tell these men that what they do is wrong. Trust me, Jefe will come."

The soldiers saw the Indians talking with Chico. "Did we give you orders to speak to them?" Diego demanded. "Don't speak unless we give you something to tell them!" And he slapped him again across the forehead before turning to mount his horse.

The slap made Chico's eyes water. As he reached up to wipe his stinging eyes, he heard one of the other captives murmur, "Look at his arm! Those are the tattoos of a strong hunter. Surely we can depend on him to help us."

Chico caught the speaker's eye and nodded very slightly. Diego glanced back but saw nothing.

They reached another river just after sunset, and Diego gave orders to make camp for the night. Once their saddles were taken off, the horses rolled on the ground, rubbing their sore backs in the soft grass. But before dawn, the soldiers saddled the horses again, roused the Indians and crossed the river.

Diego rode ahead of the group to scout for more villages to raid. Mateo and three other soldiers stayed behind to lead the captives. As he followed the soldiers around a rocky outcropping, Chico saw them stop suddenly.

In the trail stood Jefe and Estevanico—and Chico's dog.

The horses caught the dog's scent. They were jumpy, prancing nervously and bobbing their big heads. Limping, but alive, the dog was backing away from the horses when it spotted Chico. It quivered and yipped and beat its tail against Jefe's leg, but didn't approach. Jefe caught Chico's eye and smiled.

Mateo and the others were silent. Chico heard Mateo sneer, "Are these our men or savages?"

Chico gritted his teeth. "These are the men I told you about," he answered. "They're sailors from your own country."

"It's not possible. Look at them! They're filthy and ragged and nearly as naked as the natives," Mateo snorted. "I don't believe it!"

"Believe *me*, then," Jefe said in a firm voice. "I am Alvar Nuñez Cabeza de Vaca. Bring your captain to me immediately!"

Mateo's eyes grew big. Chico laughed to himself. The soldiers acted as if they'd seen a ghost.

"Of course, *Capitan*, *er, um, Señor*," Mateo stammered, his forehead wrinkled in disbelief.

"And release Chico," Jefe commanded, pointing. "He is my interpreter and a member of our party, and you have no right to hold him against his will."

Mateo started to argue, but stopped when Jefe raised one eyebrow and crossed his arms, waiting to be obeyed. Even sunburned, dirty, and barefoot, Jefe presented an air of authority.

"As you wish," Mateo said with a cocky shrug.

"Don't forget us," Chico heard the Indian next to him whisper as Mateo released Chico to join Jefe.

Once the horsemen had gone ahead on the trail to find Diego, Chico's dog leapt forward and ran to Chico. It ran with a sort of skipping motion, obviously favoring one of its hind legs. The dog's eyes were clear, but one ear was torn. Fur was missing around a gash on its head. Chico knelt to let the dog lick his face, and then looked up at Jefe.

"I'm glad you're here," he said.

"We started looking when you didn't come back," Jefe told him. "We followed the soldiers' tracks and when we found your dog whimpering and hurt at the side of the trail, we knew something bad had happened. Tell me everything."

Chico was still telling Jefe his story when Diego rode up. He stopped and stared, just as Mateo and the others had. "Can it be true?" he said with disbelief on his face.

"Of course, it's true," snapped Jefe. "If you don't

believe the word of my interpreter," he gestured at Chico, "or even your own men," he waved a hand at Mateo, "then believe the word of Alvar Nuñez Cabeza de Vaca, His Majesty's loyal servant."

"Señor, how can this be?" Diego asked, skeptical. "We thought you were dead."

"We survived a shipwreck and slavery with the help of these same natives that you have taken captive here. How dare you treat them like savages?" Jefe scolded him.

"His Majesty wants these people and this land for his empire," Diego spoke slowly and carefully as if explaining to a child. "I, too, serve the King. This is what he wants."

"His Majesty wants loyal subjects, not slaves," Jefe snapped back. "Release them at once. That is my direct command! I will be sure to tell him how his orders are being carried out when I return to his court in Spain."

Chico watched Diego go still. His eyes narrowed at Jefe's order. He lifted his chin slightly. Chico thought he saw a brief smirk, but he blinked and Diego's face was expressionless again.

"Of course, Señor de Vaca, of course," Diego answered with exaggerated politeness. "Whatever you wish." He turned to Mateo and the other soldiers. "Unbind the Indians," he ordered calmly.

He turned back to Jefe. "And of course you will need

one of my men to guide you to Culiacán, the nearest Spanish settlement," he offered.

Chico watched carefully. He didn't trust the soldier. His manners were formal, but his eyes were hard and cold. Chico thought Diego had obeyed Jefe's orders far too easily.

Jefe seemed pleased, however. "There is another outpost nearer than Pánuco? Yes, by all means, please take us there."

The released captives crowded around. One of them spoke to Chico, "What's happening? What do we do now?"

Jefe heard their questions and pulled Chico aside. "Thank them for all the care that they and the other villagers have given us. Tell them it's safe for them to go back to their homes now. They can rest easy and settle again in their villages, tilling and planting their fields as usual."

Chico stared at him. "You don't actually believe they'll be safe, do you? Don't you think the soldiers will go back and raid their villages again as soon as they can?"

Jefe looked hurt. "These are Spanish soldiers, Chico. I am a Spanish commander. I trust them to follow my orders. Don't you trust me?"

"Of course I trust you, but..." Chico argued.

"If you trust me, then you should trust them," Jefe

interrupted.

"But these soldiers aren't like you at all," Chico explained. "You heal people, and they hurt people. You walk barefoot like us, and they ride horses and carry weapons. You're as different as day and night. I trust you with my life, but I don't trust them to obey your orders."

"It's safe for the Indians to go back to their homes now, I'm telling you," Jefe insisted. "And Castillo, Dorantes, Estevanico, and I are finally on the way back to ours. Diego is even giving us a guide to lead us to the nearest settlement. That should prove to you that he can be trusted."

Chico sighed. Jefe was blind to Diego's evil intentions and it appeared that no argument was going to open his eyes. Chico decided to change the subject, but keep a close watch on Diego and the other soldiers.

"Do we leave today?" Chico asked.

"Yes, anytime. Tell them you are all free to go right away," Jefe said.

Chico shook his head. "No," he said. "I mean, when do *we* leave?"

Jefe's face fell. "Oh, Chico," he said. "We've come to the end of our journey together. I thought you understood."

"What do you mean?" Chico asked, bewildered.

"Just as soon as I get to Culiacán, I will go straight back to Spain," Jefe explained. "It's my home. It's where I belong."

Chico didn't know what to say. He didn't know what he was going to do. Things were changing too fast. "You're going all the way back to Spain?" he asked. "I thought you were going to stay in Culiacán or in Pánuco. They're Spanish settlements; they are your people. I thought that was what you were looking for."

"Oh, Chico," Jefe tried to explain. "Now that I've seen these young soldiers and how wrong they are about the best way to colonize this land, I know I have to go back to Spain and set them straight. I must explain to them about this great New World and the people who live here. I need to teach them about the things I've learned on my journey."

"I want them to understand that the people of Spain can become greater by working together with the people of the New World, not by conquering them. I want to assure the King that the best way to bring the Indians to him as loyal subjects is through kindness and cooperation."

Jefe paused and put his hand on Chico's shoulder. "I'll tell him I know it can work because we made it work. You and I. Working and traveling together, we've drawn a map for a greater empire than the King has ever imagined. I must go back to Spain and tell him these things."

Chico turned away. He couldn't look at Jefe. He had traveled with him for so long. He had depended on him. He had helped him. He had struggled alongside him. And now, their journey together was over and Jefe was leaving him. Forever. Chico hadn't realized he would never see him again. It all happened so suddenly. Chico felt blindsided–the same as he felt when the soldier's lance came out of nowhere and struck him down.

Without a word to anyone, he walked away. His dog followed him down the trail and into the woods. Chico never looked back.

Chapter 13

He and the dog walked in the direction of the river. The dog tired easily because of its lame back leg, but Chico was in no hurry. They strayed off the trail and stopped often to rest. Chico saw a couple of groups of the released captives pass on the path, but he avoided them.

He was on his own again. He crossed the river and camped there. The water was clear and sweet, and the fish were easy to trap in the shallow pools along the bank. It was a good place to rest and give the dog a chance to heal.

In the misty morning of the third day, Chico decided it was time to move on. He was anxious to return to the bison hunters' village—home—while the weather was good. It would be a long walk, and the first time he'd ever had to find his way by himself.

He whistled for his dog and set out. It was time to start his life over, again.

Down the river he heard splashing and voices, then a horse's whinny. The dog looked at Chico and whimpered. Chico pushed aside the branches that blocked his view. He saw Diego and Mateo crossing the river, and they appeared to be in a hurry. At first, Chico's only thought was to keep his distance.

Then he heard Diego shout to Mateo, "Hurry! We've almost caught up with them. The stupid savages actually thought we'd let them go!"

Mateo laughed and spurred his horse to hurry it up the bank. "We lost a lot of time because of that crazy Cabeza de Vaca. I think he lived too long with the natives and turned into one himself. Now that he's out of the way, let's see if we can get them rounded up again and then move on to other villages."

Chico's heart sank. The soldiers were going back to the same villages they'd raided before, and they weren't going to stop there. They had lied to Jefe. They would keep raiding villages and capturing Indians for slaves until the land was empty. Eventually they might even threaten Chico's new home and family. If they took Rihóy, Mica, and the others, Chico realized, it would be just like the sickness that destroyed his first home. He couldn't let that happen. The slave raiders had to be stopped.

Chico knew that the freed Indians would never suspect what was coming because Jefe had promised them it was safe to go back to their homes. And Jefe would never suspect what was happening because he was on his way back to Spain.

Chico was the only person who knew the truth. And he knew what he had to do. He had to speak for the Indians. He was the only one who could.

He turned on his heel and hurried back the direction he'd come. He didn't know if he could catch up with Jefe in time. He wasn't even sure he could find him, but he knew he had to try.

Before long, he found tracks from Jefe's group. He followed their trail for several days. He saw where they'd camped; he found torn leaves and branches where they'd broken new trail through the brush. He stopped to eat and rest only when he and the dog were too tired to continue, but the stops were short and few. Finally he came to a small Indian village.

"Have you seen any travelers, the ones who are healers?" he asked a boy who ran up when he saw Chico's dog.

The boy nodded and reached out to touch the dog's torn ear. "They were here yesterday. Three of them had beards, and one was tall and his skin was darker than a bison's hide. They carried medicine gourds, so we knew they were the healers we'd heard about. We gave them water and food but they wouldn't stay."

"Have they left already?" Chico interrupted, impatient with the boy's long answer.

The boy nodded again. "They went that way," he pointed. He started to say more, but Chico was already hurrying away, calling his thanks over his shoulder.

The sun was low when Chico caught up with them. A tall, imposing man walked beside Jefe, talking seriously. He was older than the soldiers, and he seemed to carry himself with the same calm air of authority as Jefe. When the dog spotted Jefe, it ran ahead, skipping every few steps with its back leg. Jefe felt its wet nose nudge his hand and then Chico heard him laugh.

Jefe stopped and turned around. "I think your dog will run that way for the rest of its life!" he called to Chico.

Chico hurried closer and Jefe said, "I'm glad you're here. I was sorry you left without saying good-bye." Jefe gestured to the man next to him, "Chico, this is the *alcalde*, the mayor, of Culiacan. He rules the Spanish settlement just beyond those trees. His name is Señor Diaz and he has honored us by coming to meet us."

Chico nodded his respect and quickly turned back to Jefe. He was out of breath. "The soldiers lied to you," Chico said in a rush. "They've gone back to capture the Indians again. I saw them."

Jefe looked stern. He held up his hand to slow Chico down. "Wait, Chico. Catch your breath," he advised. He glanced at the *alcalde*, who was frowning. "Señor Diaz will want to hear all about this."

Chico closed his eyes and took a deep breath, then another. He steadied himself, and started again. "The soldiers, Diego and Mateo, have gone back to raid the villages again. They are taking more villagers to sell as slaves, even though they promised you the villagers could return home safely."

The *alcalde* shook his head. "Those soldiers, especially Diego, are hotheads. I was afraid they couldn't be trusted," he said. "They have no right to raid villages and take captives, and they have no orders to do so. I've got to stop this before they cause more trouble." The *alcalde* shook his head in disgust.

He continued, "Those are peaceful Indians. We want to

work with them, not destroy them. They're the only ones who can help us learn how to live here. The land here is so different from Spain. We can't survive in the New World without their help."

"I agree. What can you do?" Jefe asked Señor Diaz.

The *alcalde* turned to Chico. "Could you show my men where Diego and his soldiers are? Would you be willing to lead them there with my orders for them to stop their raids and release any Indian captives immediately? Will you speak for me?"

Chico agreed without hesitating.

Jefe smiled. "I have an idea." He held out his walking stick with the medicine gourd tied to the top. "Take this with you," he said. "The Indians will recognize it and know they can trust you, that you truly come in peace."

The *alcalde* reached into his pocket and pulled out a small cross on a chain. "Carry this with you also," he said to Chico. "That way the soldiers will believe you speak for me, too."

Then he called to two of the lieutenants escorting the group along the road. He explained the situation.

"Bring Diego and his men directly back to Culiacan, along with any Indian leaders who are willing to come. Then together we can talk about how to live and work in peace with each other. And give Diego strictest orders that all captives," the mayor added, "are to be released. This young man will show you where to find them."

The Spanish lieutenant saluted the *alcalde*, and then turned. "Lead the way, *por favor,*" he said to Chico. "If you please," he gestured respectfully.

Chico quietly took charge and led the group back to the place where he had last seen Diego. From there, it was easy to follow the footprints of the horses. The soldiers appeared to have been in a hurry to recapture their slaves. Chico could see the careless path they had taken, leaving a trail of broken branches, trampled underbrush, and dislodged rocks. There were a couple of burned out campfires, now only cold, charred mesquite knots.

After several days on the trail, Chico and the *alcalde*'s lieutenants smelled smoke on the late afternoon breeze. Excited, they hurried forward and broke out of a dense thicket on a rise above a small valley. On the hillside below them they saw a village sitting in smoky ruins. The huts were as black as the charred mesquite knots of the old campfires they'd passed on their way. The fields, which should have been green and lush with corn and beans, were ragged patches of dry brush. And crossing the valley was a long line of brown-skinned natives, led by a uniformed soldier on horseback. Another horseman herded the group from the rear.

"That must be Diego and Mateo," Chico said, pointing. He shook his head, looking grimly past the enslaved Indians to the ruined village and dead fields.

The lieutenant looked where Chico pointed. "You know they won't be willing to surrender their slaves again, even with the *alcalde*'s orders," the soldier said quietly.

"I know," Chico reluctantly agreed. "But we can't just sit back and let them get away with it." He sighed, "The *alcalde* is very much like Jefe. They are both honorable men, and so they have a hard time understanding that sometimes others are not. Diego and Mateo just can't be trusted."

"What can we do?" the other lieutenant asked. "You're carrying our leader's token, but you're an Indian. They'll never listen to you, and we can't overpower them as long as they're on horses."

The soldier looked out at the scene below and shook his head. "This is hopeless," he said. "There's no way you're going to convince Diego to do anything he doesn't want to do." He looked at Chico who stood staring at the valley and didn't respond. "This is hopeless," the soldier repeated and started to walk away.

"Wait," Chico put up his hand to stop him. "The shape of this valley reminds me of something." He studied the landscape a moment longer. "Hmmm. It just might work," Chico said. Then he faced the two Spanish lieutenants and said, "All right. There are only three of us, so we'll have to move quickly."

The two lieutenants listened carefully as Chico explained his plan. After a few questions, they understood what he described. "And you're sure it can work?" one asked again.

"I've seen it," Chico assured him. "We can do it if we get busy."

While he made preparations, Chico kept an eye on the slave raiders' movements across the valley. "Good," he said after checking on their progress. "It looks like they've stopped to rest the horses before continuing. This is our chance; we can't waste any time. Let's get started."

The three young men each lit a torch from the small campfire they'd started. Then they separated and headed to the valley floor. Hurrying through the brush that ringed the area, they quickly touched their torches to anything that would catch fire. Soon the valley was surrounded by small blazes. The evening breezes fanned the flames, and the dry bottomland was enclosed with a ring of fire before Diego and Mateo noticed the danger.

The Indian captives began to panic. A few managed to slip away quickly through rocky gulches, scrambling just ahead of the flames that licked at their backs and singed their hair. Others, slower on their feet, stumbled across the valley searching for an escape route as the fire closed in behind them.

Diego's horse whinnied and reared and pawed the air in fear when it smelled the smoke and saw the chaos. Before Diego could catch its halter, it bolted straight for the river, where it leapt into the fast-moving water and was swept downstream. Mateo's horse followed, thundering past Diego as the trader raised his fist and screamed in frustration.

After starting the blaze, Chico and the *alcalde*'s two lieutenants met at the river where the rocky bank was free of fire. Chico and his companions waved his walking stick and called through the clouds of smoke to attract the attention of the frantic captives. The dog joined in, hopping in circles, barking and yipping with excitement. The Indians and their captors struggled to make their way to safety at the river's edge where they crouched low to catch their breath and avoid the sparks and smoke.

"You again?" Diego said in disdain when he recognized Chico. "Did that crazy Cabeza de Vaca send his native boy and his dog after me again?"

"The *alcalde* sent me," Chico answered calmly, "with orders that you are to release the captives."

"We are taking these slaves for the King!" Diego

snorted. "Why would the *alcalde* want them released?"

"Because the King doesn't need slaves," Chico explained. "Can't you see that you're stealing from the King?"

"What? You're as crazy as de Vaca!" Diego laughed.

"You're stealing the wealth of the land," Chico answered him. "You're ruining the villages and destroying the crops. You're ripping the people from their villages, and without them, the land is worthless to your King."

"These people will make valuable slaves to serve the King," Diego repeated.

"These people make this land valuable to him by remaining here," Chico said firmly. "They know how to coax the riches from the soil. They best serve the King by being caretakers of this valuable New World."

"That makes no sense!" Diego argued, shouting now.

Chico tried to explain. "Come back to Culiacán with us and let the *alcalde* explain. He has requested that the Indian leaders come also. He wants the Spanish and the natives to work out the best way to live together and serve your King."

"I refuse to take orders from a savage!" Diego bellowed.

"That is your choice to make," Chico said patiently. "Nonetheless, these Indians are free to return home to rebuild and start over. And you are free to stay here and try to survive on your own without your horse or your weapons."

With that, Chico said nothing more to Diego. Instead he turned away and approached several of the frightened Indians, showing them a path along the riverbank that would take them out of the smoky valley.

Mateo gasped. "Diego, we can't!" His eyes were wide with fear. "We'll die out here if we have to live with these savages. They hate us! I'd rather go back to Culiacán with Chico, as he suggests. At least we'll be safe there."

Diego glared scornfully at his colleague before turning to the *alcalde*'s lieutenants. "Are you so weak that you allow a savage to speak for you?" he sneered. "Are you so weak that you depend on a native to lead you? What kind of soldiers are you?" He spat at the ground in disgust.

The senior lieutenant stood tall. "I am the kind of soldier who recognizes a born leader, Diego," he said. "And it doesn't mean I'm weak when I say that this native is a stronger man than you or I could ever be. Somehow, he leads men with words and respect. He doesn't need weapons or fear."

Meanwhile, the Indian leaders had gathered around Chico. "We will be glad to go back to talk to the *alcalde* with you. There is nothing left for us here until the Spanish agree to let us live in peace again."

As the last of the captives slipped away down the river and scattered into the hills beyond, Diego watched Mateo join Chico and the lieutenants and Indian leaders. Before they began the long walk back to Culiacán, Chico turned once more to Diego.

"If you do not choose to join us, then I hope your God will have mercy on you in the wilderness, as he did Jefe," Chico told him. "Trust me; it's frightening to be helpless and alone in this land."

The group left Diego standing at the edge of the smoldering valley. As they passed over the last ridge, Chico glanced back, but he couldn't make out anything through the haze.

Days later, they arrived back at the settlement, dirty and exhausted, but proud. The *alcalde* welcomed each man, native and Spanish, warmly and with equal respect.

Spotting Chico in the group, Jefe pulled him aside. "We waited for you," he said. "Now that you're back, Señor Diaz will settle these problems between the soldiers and the Indians. And then I want you to go on to Spain with us."

Chico said nothing.

"You were right. You saw what I refused to see," Jefe continued. "I shouldn't have trusted Diego. I want you to travel home with me to Spain. It would be a great adventure for you, plus I could use your help when I talk to the King about colonizing the New World. By meeting you, he'd see for himself that the natives aren't savages."

Chico smiled. His dog leaned against his leg. "No, you were right before, Jefe," he said. "I shouldn't go with you."

Jefe started to protest, but Chico held up a hand to stop him. "I don't belong there."

"But do you really belong here?" Jefe asked as Estevanico walked over to join them.

Chico smiled at Estevanico and then answered Jefe. "Yes, I do. This is my land. My home is here. My family is here. They are my people, and they'll need my help if your world and my world are going to grow together.

"I've seen the best and the worst of your people and of mine. I've known kindness and captivity from both. I've been treated with both respect and cruelty. I've survived illness and abuse. I've watched magical healings and seen inside a man's chest. I've learned languages and medicine from both the Spanish and the Indians.

"I've glimpsed both worlds, Jefe. And they're both changing."

Chico drew a deep breath and stood tall. He looked Jefe in the eye and said, "As people from your world join people from my world, I want to be the leader who helps them find their way together. This is where I belong."

His eyes bright, Estevanico wrapped his strong arms around Chico, stepped back, and said simply, "Be safe." He knelt and scratched the dog's head before leaving Jefe and Chico alone again.

Jefe said nothing for a moment. He swallowed.

"I envy the man who calls you his son," Jefe said in a hoarse voice. Then he reached out and grasped Chico's arm. "Until we meet again," he said, "in this world or the next."

With Jefe's walking stick in one hand and the dog by his side, Chico started to the meetinghouse where the *alcalde* and the Indian leaders waited. Together they would work out a way to live in peace and make this New World a place where all could enjoy the riches that the land offered.

When he reached the door of the meetinghouse, Chico paused to look back.

He couldn't see Jefe against the glare of the sunset, but he knew he'd be watching. Chico raised the walking stick high in salute. Then he turned to help the others find their way.